CONTENTS

Careers Uncovered guides aim to expose the truth about what it's really like to work in a particular field, containing unusual and thought-provoking facts about the profession you are interested in. Written in a lively and accessible style, *Careers Uncovered* guides explore the highs and lows of the career, along with the job opportunities and skills and qualities you will need to help you make your way forward.

Titles in this series include:

About the Author

Andi Robertson was born in South Devon in 1959 and educated at Kingsbridge School. After 22 years of sales and management experience in London and Devon, having formed his own marketing and sales consultancy business in 1982, he opted for a change of career and obtained a BA(Hons) degree and the Certificate of Education. This enabled him to become a business adviser and trainer with local enterprise agencies, to lecture at Plymouth College of Further Education for the Chartered Institute of Marketing and to work as a marketing consultant. Since 2003 Andi has also written articles on marketing and small business topics for regional newspapers and national magazines.

Acknowledgements

Andi would like to acknowledge:

- The support of his wife Jane

- The help of his assistant Debbie Hamilton

- Enterprise Plymouth Ltd and the *Evening Herald* for allowing him to reproduce material in this book

- All the clients and colleagues and friends who have contributed to this book.

Collin's Dictionary defines self-employment as 'earning one's living in one's own business or through freelance work rather than as an employee of another'. Working for yourself can be a challenging and rewarding experience. It enables you to dictate the pace and the direction of your own business and to be your own boss, which can bring a new sense of freedom to how you live your life.

The choice is yours and the world is your oyster. You could be anything from a plumber to a ballet teacher; accountant to a demolition expert; window cleaner to a solicitor. You could earn as little as you need or as much as you dream of. The world of self-employment has no boundaries. You are limited only by what you put into your business in terms of energy and determination.

THE SCOPE OF THIS BOOK

There are many different kinds of self-employment. Picture your local doctor getting his car repaired. The doctor may have a partnership in a busy local practice and the mechanic may operate as a 'one man band' from a small lock-up around the corner. Both are self-employed. So are dentists and so are barristers. And then, of course, there are those people who can afford to buy another company and take it over. Since there are very established training routes to careers such as barrister and doctor, and since only those with a serious

> amount of cash will be able to buy an existing company,
> however, this book will focus on working for yourself by
> starting up your own business.

Working for yourself opens up an extraordinary range of options.
You can become anything that takes your fancy; the only obligation
you have to yourself (and your bank balance) is that this exercise is
a profitable one – and it might help if you enjoy it!

With that it mind, it is not surprising that increasing numbers of
people are setting up in business; self-employment is a sector that
the Government wishes to encourage as much as possible, because
it employs people and pays taxes – and that's good for UK
businesses.

FASCINATING FACTS

**Last year, The Prince's Trust helped 12,793 young
entrepreneurs set up in business.**

There are therefore many organisations out there willing to help the
aspiring entrepreneur realise their ambitions – from the Young
Enterprise scheme in school to Business Link organisations and
The Prince's Trust. All you have to do is come up with your business
idea and persuade people that you can make it work.

But that's easier said than done. Where do you start? The idea of
setting up your own business can seem daunting and complicated.
What does it take to make it work? What sort of a person do you
have to be? What do you need to know? *Working for Yourself* will
answer these and many more questions, providing a positive no-
nonsense guide to what it is like to be self-employed and how you
go about becoming one of the UK's many entrepreneurs. It's packed
with facts and tips as well as case studies, checklists to help keep
you on track and quizzes to help you measure your own attitudes
and aspirations

The first chapter looks at the idea of self-employment in more detail, exploring what entrepreneurs love about their work and explaining some terms you will come across. There's also a quiz to help you decide whether you've got what it takes to succeed as an entrepreneur. Because there are no hard-and-fast rules about what specific skills you need or what entry routes there are, the next part of the book takes a broad approach, looking at the key stages that you need to go though to set up a business:

● Proper planning – conducting research, writing a business plan

● Promoting your business – how to sell your product or service

● Keeping customers

● Successful staff – how you go about taking on your first employee

● Other stuff – where to look for funding and what rules and regulations have to be dealt with.

The information in these chapters should provide you with not only a useful reference point, but also with a taste of the kind of work you'll be doing and the kind of problems you might come across – and all this will help you get an idea of whether self-employment is really going to be your cup of tea. Chapter 7 then looks at some of the training opportunities available to prepare you for the world self-employment. And finally, the Resources section at the end of the book will direct you to the many organisations that are ready and waiting to help you become self-employed.

This book aims to open doors of opportunity for the reader. Don't forget, the choice is yours – and if you do take the plunge, becoming an entrepreneur could be something you will never regret. The case study below should give you a taster of what happens when your business takes off – it should whet your appetite, as well as giving you a bit of warning of some of the problems you might encounter.

THERESA'S STORY

Theresa set her business up when she was 23 with her partner, Jason. They now employ six people based at their home. Here is her story.

We are here today to talk about your thriving business. But perhaps you could take us back to the beginning of the business and how you came to get the whole thing underway.

'Jason, my partner suggested we should try setting up on our own, so we started to think about how we should go about it. We looked around for small business advice courses to get basic advice on where to start running our own business.

'We went to an Enterprise Agency; at that time they ran an eight-day course that looked at marketing, finance and various other issues. It gave a basic insight into how to run a business and the legalities involved. It gave us a good basis on where to go from there. Without it I wouldn't have had the first idea on how to start.'

You had better now tell us, before we go any further, what the business is.

'We supply, deliver and install garage doors, doors, roller shutters, industrial doors and windows. Most of the garage doors are for the domestic market, but we also supply a lot of commercial customers with roller shutters and industrial doors. We have some quite big contracts with local councils for schools and banks.'

Is this what Jason did before you started out on your own?

'Yes. Jason was employed for 15 years, so he knew the business. I knew nothing about it other than what he had told me. I was experienced in admin so we decided to become a team, with Jason handling the practical issues and me looking after the admin. I kept my job with Toshiba for a year after we started trading until we felt confident enough for me to commit full time.'

So you made a couple of wise moves – firstly, you knew the business inside out because Jason had worked in the trade for 15 years, and secondly you didn't cut off your income from other sources straight away, so you had something to fall back on.

'No – mainly because I was on good money at Toshiba and I knew when we sat down and calculated all the ingoings and outgoings that I could afford to pay the mortgage if we didn't make any money from the business.'

What do you think you got right at the beginning?

'I think we were very lucky in that initially we had a lot of contacts in the business. Jason knew a lot of people. We have been very fortunate that, even up until this year, the beginning of our fourth year of trading, we have only ever advertised in the *Yellow Pages* – all other work has come to us via word of mouth.'

So knowing your market before you made the jump is quite crucial, because having lots of contacts is very important in providing you with a broad base of different streams of income. What else did you do right at the beginning?

'I tried to get as much help and advice as I could.'

You went out looking for help?

'Yes. Jason's parents had a good friend who had run a business doing exactly the same thing and had retired 18 months previously. We went to them on numerous occasions as he knew how the business went. Just not being afraid to ask people was the main thing – not feeling that our questions were silly, but more that they were important.'

When you started up in business did you buy all new kit?

'No'

You were cautious?

'Yes. We probably made fewer mistakes because we were cautious. We shopped around for the van and insurance. We bought the minimum amount of company uniform that we could get away with.

'There are certain things you can scrimp on – I have learned the hard way that you can't scrimp on a really good computer! But I picked the office furniture up really cheaply in a second-hand store as bankrupt stock. I bought the desk and chair for £1 each! Some people would, but if you are like me don't spend a fortune carpeting it all out and making it look lovely because there are probably more important things to spend your money on.'

Do you have a lock-up where you store all your stuff?

'We've got three now, all in different places. It is slightly complicated for me as well as I am never quite sure which lock-up things are in. The amount of time I spend driving from lock-up to lock-up!'

How did the first year go?

'The first year there was enough business to keep Jason going. I would come home from work in the evenings and take over doing the paperwork and the invoicing.'

A tricky balance, holding down a job and coming home to more work in the evenings. Do you think it was the right thing to do?

'Yes, definitely. It was a lot of hard work for that year; I'd be finishing one job and then coming home and starting another one. For the first six months it was tricky, but it was new and exciting. After the first six months we started getting busier – there was too much work for Jason to cope with and then, of course, the extra admin work was putting more pressure on me. By the end of the first year I was happy to give up my day job and concentrate on the office work here, luckily I was made redundant.'

So you made the big leap from a paid job into self-employment. Did you at some point take on a new member of staff?

'At that time we took on an apprentice. Although we could have done with an experienced engineer at that time, we didn't want to take one on because of the extra cost incurred and we didn't know if there was going to be enough work.'

Another balancing act?

'Yes; I think they never stop. Even now, although our guys are absolutely flat out, we still keep asking ourselves whether there is enough work to take us through. You either play it safe or you take risks.'

So we've looked at some of things you did right – but what did you do wrong?

'Oh, I'm sure we made hundreds of mistakes. We try not to make them, particularly where health and safety and the law are concerned – but we've made plenty of little errors. For example, to still be working from home as we are now is a mistake because it interferes constantly with the rest of our lives. We've lost our dining room to the business and Jason's two children come home from school and have to tiptoe around if I have a meeting with someone. Use of the phone for personal chats is also restricted. It is hard for the children as we never turn off. I have a friend who likes to pop in for a cup of tea; I find I can't spare the time as I am trying to work.

'We thought about taking on premises but didn't want to because we couldn't afford the risk of going bankrupt; we didn't want to take too much on at the beginning. We should have thought about getting outside premises before now. Another problem is all this paperwork – I need someone to come and help me.'

Why haven't you done that?

'Because I don't want some else working in my home. The other disadvantage of working from home is that if I have business callers (like customers or reps) I'll spend about an hour tiding up before they are due to arrive.

'We are now looking for premises, which is taking longer than we had hoped. We had an opportunity 18 months ago, which we turned down. Hindsight is a wonderful thing!'

Any other errors?

'Probably another disadvantage of working from home is the danger of getting too friendly with staff. You don't mean to. There is a thin line which is crossed as staff come into your home, chat to the children and start to become part of the family.

That's a common problem. Maintaining a professional distance when first employing people is difficult anyway, particularly when you are young and want to get on with everybody. It tends to cause difficulties.

'Yes. There has to be a line between I am your boss and you are the employee.'

So you have to approach the employee/employer relationship carefully and set parameters and control how far you are prepared to take the social side of it.

'Yes, definitely.'

Anything else?

'The bank. This will sound strange but when we first started I went for the bank with the lowest charges. When we were a sole trader (we became limited after one year) they were great but we found we couldn't do anything in the branch.'

You mean you need a direct access to your manager, rather than central customer lines?

'You need to be able to go into the bank and draw cash out over the counter, because you never know if something could happen to your cash card. We were stuck without our cash card for five days until a new one was issued. It is just something I would never have thought of. It is handy to have someone there you can talk to either in the branch or over the phone.'

So your relationship with the bank is important. Is it the same with accountants and other professionals?

'Yes. Cheap is not always better – that is what I finally worked out!'

Tell us a little bit about how the business developed in the second, third and fourth years.

'In the second year the apprentice unfortunately had to leave us. After that Jason's dad came on board to work for us, making it more of a family affair. It was a really good thing for us certainly, but he would work 80–90 hours a week, including evenings and weekends, for next to nothing. This was great for us at that stage, as we were trying to build up the business – but we felt bad. Employing family can sometimes have its downfalls. If he ever did a job wrong, he took it really personally and felt he had let us down. We knew he hadn't.

So if you involve members of the family you have to approach this with a degree of care. What happened next?

'In the third year we got an engineer on board and Jason's dad left shortly after that. At the end of the second year we took on another apprentice and at the start of the third year there were four of us. Now in total there are six.

'We have two teams of door fitters – Andy and his apprentice, and Mike and his apprentice. We do 24-hour call-out seven days a week, as we have to be there within four hours. Jason does everything else.

Is the four hour attendance written in to your contracts?

'No, but we can't afford not to abide by that with the bigger contracts such as with the Post Office or a Bank. Our customers rely on that and know that we will be there.'

That sounds like quite a responsibility. How do you protect your family life?

'I don't think we really do. That is a whole issue. Hopefully within a year we shall have business premises and things are going to be so, so different. You get to the stage when you get a bit disheartened and down about it. You seem to be doing the same thing day in and day out without reaping any benefits. After a while you forget the benefits you had in the beginning.'

This can be a problem with a business. You managed the formative years of the business and have lost control of the growth!

'Yes the business just completely runs us. I think, basically, we need to sit down and decide where we need to go. What do we want to do? We need to give the business some direction. And learn to say no!'

You mean you need to reassert control?

'Yes. I think it is all a learning curve and you've got to realise that you have got to where you are now, you've done so well that you've got to put your foot down and say "it is my business and this is what I am going to do".'

So what would you say are the main advantages of running your own business?

'Well, being your own boss. We've got a nice car. We can afford to pay for the house. We don't really think about money, and we don't have worries about money or redundancy.

And what are the disadvantages?

'We don't get to go on holiday because we're on a 24-hour call-out seven days a week.'

To round off the interview, can you give some top tips to aspiring entrepreneurs?

'I would advise them to think very carefully – certainly a lot more carefully that we did. You do need to think and get a lot of support from your family and other people around you, like the enterprise agency.

'Where finances are concerned, keep expenditure to a minimum. Obviously don't scrimp on things that you really do need (like the computer). Don't go out and buy things that you really don't need at that time.

'I'd like to advise people not to borrow money, but that is highly unlikely for most people. We were fortunate in that we borrowed money from the family and we paid that back after the first year, so we don't have an overdraft. But don't borrow more than the absolute minimum.

If you want something, wait until you have enough money to buy it rather than buying on credit. Paying interest can cause a lot of stress and there is enough stress already when you are running your own business.

'Think very carefully where your family are concerned, certainly if you have young children. Think about getting that balance right.'

Perhaps now that the business is at that crossroads that is one of the considerations you would take into account? Re-assessing what you are going to do with the business, ie moving into commercial property, delegate and create time so you can make positive adjustments to your personal lives?

'Yes, that is what we want, to finish work at five or six o'clock or whenever it may be and still have a happy medium.'

You mean, now the business has moved on beyond the start-up phase, you must manage its growth, rather than letting the growth manage you.

'Exactly.'

CHAPTER 1

Getting started

GET INSPIRED

Self-employment makes a significant contribution to the economic health of the United Kingdom. Around 7.5% of the total UK population is self-employed, yet these 8 million entrepreneurs are responsible for a healthy 12% of the countries total earnings (GDP). Just look at the box below to see what you can achieve with a little determination and flair.

SUCCESS STORIES

Here are some of the UK's most successful entrepreneurs:

- **Richard Branson**: Aged 55. Founded Virgin Records in 1972. Sold in 1992 for £500m

- **James Murray Wells**: Aged 22. Founded Glasses Direct in 2004. Turnover £5m

- **Liz Jackson**: Aged 25. Founded Great Guns Marketing 1998. Turnover £2m. Growth rate 40% per annum

---

- **Anita Roddick**: Aged 64. Founded The Body Shop in 1976. Sold to L'Oreal in 2006 in a deal worth £652m. Made a Dame of the British Empire in 1998

- **Stelios Haji-Ioannou**: Aged 39. Chairman of Easyjet. A serial entrepreneur who has established more than 16 ventures, the first of which, Stelmar Shipping, was an oil tanker business. It floated on the New York Stock Exchange in 2001 for approx £1.3 billion.

FASCINATING FACTS

According to a report carried out by the University of Durham, 'the self-employed work longer hours for lower wages than their wage-slave counterparts', partly due to concern about their future financial security. However, the increased flexibility and independence that self-employment offers more than compensates, and they are happier than those employed by others.

Source: *Daily Mail*, April 2006

Self-employment has a unique set of advantages over employment. Here is what some successful entrepreneurs had to say about what they liked about running their own business:

- 'I love the fact that I can work at my own pace and not the boss's.'

- 'I love being in control of my own destiny and not having others make decisions about my future.'

- 'When I get up and walk into a busy office and workshop, it gives me a sense of achievement because I started it all.'

- 'I enjoy reaping 100% of the rewards for the efforts I have put into my work and not having to share them with the boss.'

- 'I can decide when I am going on holiday. I don't have to ask anyone's permission.'

- 'My business is my hobby. I love my hobby. Does it get any better than that?'

- 'I work to live and my business allows me time to enjoy my family and leisure time.'

If hearing these things whets your appetite for going it alone, great – but there's a big difference between having a business idea and actually making it work. You'll need the personal attributes and determination to get things going, as well as a knowledge of the business environment in which you now operate and the processes you must go through to get funding and to make sure you comply with all the rules and regulations. This chapter will help you decode some of the business language you may come across, and outline some of the characteristics of the successful entrepreneur.

GET THE LINGO

One of the things that can confuse people about business is the jargon. Sometimes there is a perception that business people use over-complicated words to dress up simple ideas and make them sound better. It is certainly true that business is full of jargon – but often the words used are quite technical and refer to specific business situations and processes, which you need to understand. For instance, did you know that there are more than five different kinds of business status? Have a look at the jargon buster below to find out more.

JARGON BUSTER

BUSINESS STATUS

Sole trader – one person owning and operating a business

Partnership – business owned by two or more people

Self-employment – a sole trader or partners in a partnership, but not a limited company

Limited liability partnership – two or more people as a partnership having limited liability for the debts of the business

Limited company – separate legal entity registered at Companies House limiting the personal liability of its officers

Co-operative – an association of people who collectively own and control a business

FINANCE

Income Tax – tax paid on profit

National Insurance Contribution (NIC) – amount paid (based on earnings) for state services like NHS, state pensions etc

Self-assessment – being self-employed means that you are responsible for submitting your own tax return

Value-added tax (VAT) – tax due on goods sold once annual turnover of the business has reached £61,000 (figure correct in April 2006)

Business rates – council tax for a business premises

SUPPORT

Enterprise Agency – local agency providing free business advice and support to start-ups and small businesses

Business Link – national organisation providing advice, support and information to all existing businesses

Business Support Agencies – agencies that provide business advice, support and information

INSURANCE, SAFETY AND REGULATIONS

Buildings insurance – an insurance taken out by payment of a premium to ensure funds can become available should buildings be damaged or destroyed

Public liability – an insurance taken out by payment of a premium to ensure funds can become available for a member of the public should he or she be injured or killed by fault of the business owner

Employers' liability – an insurance taken out by payment of a premium to ensure funds can become available for a member of staff should he or she be injured or killed by fault of the business owner

Professional indemnity – an insurance taken out by payment of a premium to ensure funds can become available for anyone who suffers loss of business by fault of the person providing the service

Health and Safety Executive (HSE) – responsible for health and safety regulation in UK to protect people's health and safety in the workplace

Planning permission – permission granted, usually by a Local Authority, to ensure premises are only used for the registered purposes

MAKING MONEY

Unique selling point (USP) – The aspect of your business that makes you 'stand out from the crowd'

Referral – a customer who has been directed to you by a third party

SWOT analysis – an analysis of strengths, weaknesses, opportunities and threats relating to yourself, your business and your competitors

> **Cash flow forecast** – an essential document showing the forecast flow of funds in and out of the business on a month-by-month basis
>
> **Profit and loss statement (P&L)** – a forecast of figures taken from the cash flow forecast at the beginning of each year of trading

GET THE MINDSET

The specific skills you will need to make a success of your business will vary hugely depending on what sector you are in. If you plan to launch a business as a hairdresser then clearly you will need hairdressing skills; if you plan to sell skateboards on the internet, then being able to cut people's hair is not going to be a whole lot of use! However, there are some core qualities that all entrepreneurs need to succeed. Of course you'll need to be knowledgeable about and skilled in your chosen sector. You'll also need to have a good grasp of figures and of English, or to know someone who can help you with these things – many people have overcome all sorts of personal barriers to become successful entrepreneurs – for example, one individual was diagnosed with Multiple Sclerosis but actually turned this to her advantage by setting herself up as a commercial disability awareness trainer. Beyond this, you'll need to be:

- Organised

- Motivated

- Determined

- Resourceful

- Ambitious

- Energetic.

When you start up your company it's likely that you'll be the only member of staff, or at least be the head of a very small team. That means you'll have to fulfil all the roles that, in a larger company, would be performed by all sorts of specialists. You'll be:

- Carrying out market research

- Presenting to investors

- Organising publicity and sales campaigns

- Presenting to clients

- Doing admin and accounting

- Managing any staff you have.

Handling such a diverse set of responsibilities means you'll need to be extremely flexible, adaptable and able to learn quickly. Take a read through Chapters 2–6 of this book to get an idea of the kind of things you will be doing, and think about how you'll cope when the buck stops with you – for everything.

Remember, working for yourself is exactly that – you have to be your own boss, and that is not always easy. There'll be no one to crack the whip or moan at you if you're late – and equally, there'll be no one to share your frustration when things don't go according to plan. Being self-employed is a mindset – you need an extremely responsible, controlled, pro-active and positive attitude to make things work. Take the look at the following quiz to see if self-employment is likely to suit you (and you are likely to suit it!).

QUIZ

Answer 'A', 'B' or 'C' to each of the following questions:

1. **How would you feel if you had to work late?**
   a) OK – I want to give 110% to the job
   b) Only if I had to
   c) No way – I would only want to work within the hours of my contract

2. **How well do you get on with people in authority (eg your boss)?**
   a) Not very well – I think I could do better
   b) I get on well with people and would want to work as a team
   c) I rely on others totally to tell me what to do

3. **Are you tidy when working?**
   a) Yes – everything is in its place
   b) Sometimes, but things can go missing
   c) No – I don't even think about it

4. **How do you prioritise your work?**
   a) Prepare a daily schedule and work to it
   b) List important tasks and remember the rest
   c) Deal with issues as and when

5. **How do you cope with several tasks at once?**
   a) I deal with the important ones first
   b) Select the one that interests me first
   c) Make several starts on various tasks and continue with the easiest one

6. **How do you cope with unexpected problems?**
   a) Carefully and systematically
   b) Use my experience with similar problems in the past
   c) I am no good at dealing with unexpected difficulties and try to pass them to someone else

7. **Are you a team member?**
    a) No – I work better on my own
    b) Sometimes, but I can work on my own if necessary
    c) Yes – I enjoy team games and like to work with others

8. **Do you like your work colleagues/school friends/teachers/lecturers?**
    a) I tolerate them but keep myself to myself
    b) Yes – but I keep a distance whilst remaining friendly
    c) Very much – I enjoy the camaraderie

9. **What do you think about delegation?**
    a) I think it is 'passing the buck' and I would rather do it myself
    b) Sometimes it's a necessary process, particularly if I am to learn more
    c) I think it's very useful to pass on a task if you can't do it yourself

What's your result?

Now add up your score, awarding yourself the following points for each answer you made:

'A' = 1 point
'B' = 2 points
'C' = 3 points

If you got 9–14 points …
… you might be suited to self-employment as you like to work independently and are self-motivated. But beware; you could overwork yourself and you must make sure you plan enough free time to relax and switch off. You also need to be careful not to become isolated, so you will need to keep networking and keep in touch with contacts and colleagues.

If you got 15–22 points …
… your balanced attitude should make you suited to self-employment, but you must plan your business carefully and remember to prioritise and be methodical.

If you got 23–27 points ...
... you enjoy the company of your colleagues at work and appreciate the fact that there is a support network for you – both personally and professionally. You should think very carefully before entering self-employment and will have to work on your self-discipline. There's a danger that you may feel lonely and you may not enjoy dealing with the problems you'll face. If you do decide to become self-employed, make sure you build a strong network of colleagues.

GET AN IDEA

The chances are, if you're reading this book you already have some idea of what service or product your business might provide. For many, having the basic idea is the easy bit – it's fleshing it out into something profitable that can be a challenge. If this sounds familiar, read on – the next section gives an overview of the different places you can look for information, support and funding.

If you're not yet sure what your business might do then it's time to get thinking. Here are a few questions to ask yourself:

- What do you like doing?

- What do you know most about?

- What are the characteristics of your area? (eg is there a good tourist trade? What do the majority of people like doing?)

- Have you ever found yourself thinking 'I could do that so much better'...?

- Have you ever heard friends or acquaintances repeatedly moaning about a certain service, product or lack thereof?

Brainstorm your answers down on a piece of paper, and look at places where your answers to some of the questions overlap. If you get really stuck, have a look at a business directory like the *Yellow Pages* to get an idea of what's out there, and browse the internet.

> ## FASCINATING FACTS
>
> **Construction is the most popular industry for self-employment – 20% of all those who are self-employed work in this area. Other popular sectors are Banking, finance and insurance (19%), Distribution, hotels and restaurants (19%) and Public administration, education and health (10%).**
> **Source: Office for National Statistics, Labour Force Survey**

GET HELP

If you've read through this chapter and think that you have what it takes, then next thing you need to do is some serious research. In fact, you've already started, by reading this book – but there are also plenty of organisations out there offering expert advice and information.

For the initial research stage, there are a number of websites offering guidance for start-ups – for example, www.startups.co.uk and www.startinbusiness.co.uk. Once your plans are more developed, organisations like Business Link, Chamber of Commerce and your local Enterprise agency may well be able to offer advice and support, and the Department of Trade and Industry (DTi) will also refer you to local initiatives for the small business sector.

There is strong encouragement for the enterprise sector to flourish from EU, national and regional governments. Self-employed people pay taxes and employ people – and politicians need businesses doing both these things.

> ## FASCINATING FACTS
>
> **Chancellor of the Exchequer Gordon Brown is strongly in favour of entrepreneurship. In June 2000, he said: 'Enterprise for all in every region should be a reality, not a dream – so that anyone who seriously wants to start a business can get the advice and help they need'.**

> He went on to say that everyone should have the opportunity to 'start a business, to become self-employed, upgrade their skills and rise as far as their talents and potential can take them' and foresaw 'a Britain where there is not just a narrow ladder of opportunity but a broad and expansive highway of opportunity for all'.

A good way of measuring the Government's real attitude towards entrepreneurship is to see if they put their money where their mouth is – in other words, is there evidence of practical help for the self-employed sector in the UK? Well actually, there is help out there, although it varies from area to area. Organisations like The Prince's Trust offer funding, and Government departments like the Small Business Service (SBS) have also been set up to make sure that Government support services (including access to finance) are accessible, relevant and of high quality.

You will find contact details of all the organisations mentioned in this section at the back of the book in the Resources section.

GET GOING

So you've got an idea, you've done some initial research and you think you've got what it takes to make it work. What now? The next five chapters of this book give you a step-by-step guide to initiating and developing your business – from researching your business plan to managing expansion and staff. Read on …

CHAPTER 2

Proper planning

Let's assume that you have a product or service in mind for a new business start up. You can't wait to get going and your family and friends think it's a wonderful idea. What's your next step? Well, the first thing you should do is pause for a moment. It's not surprising that you're keen; it is your 'baby' after all, and your family and friends are bound to be positive are they not? Proper planning is crucial if the pitfalls that await the newly self-employed business person are to be avoided. This chapter will look at the research you need to do, and how to incorporate it into a business plan which you can then use to get funding. The legalities checklist on pages 42–44 offers a handy guide to the steps you need to take in the first few months of trading.

LOOKING BEFORE YOU LEAP

Perhaps one of the most important things to consider in the early stages is the matter of research. The business start-up is often the realisation of a long-held ambition, so it is not surprising that people are keen to get on with it and can be reluctant to take time out to conduct research. But it is wise to delay the launch of your business and conduct research before taking on financial commitments such as a lease for premises or a loan to buy equipment or print stationary – this can seem frustrating, but it's worth it in the long run. Frequently, taking the time to 'look before you leap' has uncovered time-consuming and costly issues that could otherwise have killed the business off in its infancy. The next paragraphs look at what research you should be doing, and how you can go about carrying it out.

WHAT IS RESEARCH FOR?

One of the best definitions of marketing is 'finding out what customers want, then setting out to meet their needs, providing it can be done at a profit. Marketing includes market research, pricing, advertising, distribution and selling'. This definition rather neatly illustrates what you should think about when you consider what research you need to do during the initial planning stage of your business start-up.

Research should be a cost-effective way of finding out what people believe, think, want and need or do. You can find these things out by reading research that has already been done (known as secondary research) or by doing the research yourself (known as primary research).

There are three principal groups of people who should be researched carefully before you launch your business: competitors, suppliers and customers. Gaining a thorough knowledge of each group will lessen the chances of making a mistake and increase your chances of creating a successful and, above all, profitable business. So what questions should you be asking each group, and how do you go about finding the answers?

SOME QUESTIONS FOR YOUR COMPETITORS

Your competitors will be good at some things and bad at others. They may have been doing what you hope to do for some years, so you may have quite a lot to learn from them. For obvious reasons, some of the competition may not be willing to talk or help you set up your business, but others – perhaps those who live some distance away and don't see you as potential competition – may be delighted to help. The knowledge gained from these people could prove to be invaluable, even if you have to buy them lunch in Land's End or John O'Groats! Here are some of the things you should be asking them:

- Does anyone else make a similar product or offer a similar service?

- How much do they sell it for?

- Where do they sell it?

- What other products do they sell?

- What is the standard of quality offered?

- What are their unique selling points?

SOME QUESTIONS FOR YOUR SUPPLIERS

Manufacturing, service and creative start-ups all need to know where their raw materials are coming from – whether these be steel, lawnmowers or oil paints. The companies who supply you with these raw materials are known as your suppliers, and you need to explore the efficiency of potential suppliers and the quality of their goods and service. Continuity of supply and 'quality control' are both crucial matters that must not be left to chance and deserve to be fully examined at outset. You need to think about who you will use and have an awareness of what this will cost, and any other complications. Start by asking *yourself*:

- What do you need in terms of equipment and materials?

- Can you choose your supplier or are you restricted to one?

- Where will you get them?

Once you have an idea of what you need and how much, approach potential suppliers to find out the following information:

- What price will be charged?

- Is the price easily affected by changes in the marketplace?

- What payment terms are offered? (These are important for cash flow)

- What are the minimum order quantities?

- What is the reputation of your proposed suppliers?

SOME QUESTIONS FOR YOUR CUSTOMERS

Your customers are arguably the most important group that should be looked at in-depth before you venture forth on your journey towards a self-employed future. You must know before you start up your business what your customers expect, who they are buying from at the moment and what they think about your proposed product or service. If you manage to develop an understanding of your future customer base's expectations and needs, you will have an improved chance of identifying how to meet demand efficiently and profitably. You need to find answers to the following questions:

- Do they want the product or service?

- Where would they expect to buy the product or service?

- How much would they be prepared to pay?

- Who would they buy for?

- Where have they bought this product or service in the past?

- What were their likes/dislikes?

HOW DO YOU CONDUCT RESEARCH?

As mentioned at the beginning of this chapter, there are two kinds of research – primary and secondary. General sources of secondary research (ie research which has already been carried out by others) include:

- **Business Link** and **other support agencies** – eg Enterprise Agencies providing advice and guidance to start-up and small businesses covering, for example, health and safety as well as industry-specific information on different types of business (eg plumbing, retail etc)

- **Business information factsheets (BIFs)** – produced by a company called Cobweb, these factsheets provide business advisers and their small business clients with a practical range of business management guides and how-to checklists covering over 300 topics including business start-up, small business finance, trading legally, using IT and the internet, exporting and importing, finding new customers and business admin

- Ask about Cobweb factsheets at your local Enterprise Agency

- **Chambers of commerce** – regional branches of the British Chamber of Commerce, providing a comprehensive range of relevant, cost-effective, value-added business services, specifically geared to the needs of the business community

- **Government** – eg National Statistics Online (www.statistics.gov.uk) and the Small Business Service

- **Media** – eg national and regional newspapers, TV, radio

- **Internet**.

Alternatively you could visit your local library's reference section, where a wealth of national and regional information on every imaginable subject is freely available. Newsagents and bookshops will also stock all sorts of publications that may well be of use to you whatever your chosen business. It is also likely that there will be more specialised organisations offering in-depth information about your chosen sector – although obviously the organisations that are of use to you will depend on what product you plan to sell. Take a look at the list below to give you some ideas.

- **Trade associations** – eg a prospective retailer could get information from the British Shops and Stores Association

- **Trade magazines** – eg a prospective egg distributor could read *Poultry International* magazine

- **Councils** – eg district councils

- **Professional bodies** – eg tourist boards (which have regional branches providing marketing advice for UK tourist businesses), the Law Society, National Federation of Builders

- **Consumer organisation** – eg *Which?* magazine

- **Suppliers** – could be a good source of information on market trends

- **Competitors** – who are, of course after the same customers!

Carrying out your own primary research is more complicated and time-consuming – but it gives results that you know are directly relevant to your product and your location. Here are some methods of carrying out primary research:

- **Focus groups** – exploring/recording a group's beliefs and opinions; best used with potential customers. See box below for more detail

- **One-to-one interviews** – best used with competitors and potential customers

- **Questionnaires and surveys** – a series of questions for potential customers about what sort of service they would like to get out of your business and what gaps they think there are in the marketplace; can be carried out on paper, by telephone review or on the street

- **Footfall counts** – recording number of people passing a certain point, eg visitors to a shop

- **Product sampling** – testing customer responses

- **Observation checklist** – a record of what you have seen when you visited competitors.

Only someone with a serious amount of time on their hands would have the time to pursue all these avenues of research. What's important is that you take the time to decide which kinds of research are going to be most effective for your business. For example, imagine for a moment that you are an aspiring florist. Having considered the above research options, you may feel that you will be able to best learn more about your competition by observing all of your competitors using a checklist including the following points:

● What do they sell besides flowers?

● What market do they serve?

● What do they charge for a dozen roses?

● Does the staff wear a uniform?

● What did you like or dislike about their service?

You could then put together a focus group to find out more about what your customers want, and visit the local library to check out available information on florist industry trends in the UK.

SPOTLIGHT ON FOCUS GROUPS
How to form a focus group
A focus group is a group of 6–10 typical customers, colleagues or friends, gathered together under the direction of a group leader. The purpose of the group is to discuss their reactions to a product or service, and for their responses to be used to inform the business planning process. There are some important rules to observe for a focus group:

● The group leader must set out some good, focused, unbiased questions if the analysis is to be of use and the answers reliable

● The group must be objective and prepared to be honest

● The group leader is *not* a participant; his or her job is to chair the meeting, outline structure and purpose and ensure that the group stays on track. It is best if the leader sits apart from the group and observes, taking notes for later analysis, and it is imperative that he or she refrains from arguing with the participants when they are critical!

● Non-verbal responses should be noted, which is why these sessions are often videoed and each participant's notes and jottings retained

● Remember, you don't want your ideas falling into the wrong hands so take advice and use a confidentiality agreement if you need to.

How focus groups can help – real-life story
An artist had met with some success selling her work to the extent that she decided to give up her day job and change her painting from a hobby to a business. Her work ranged from abstract to landscape and she had decided to concentrate on the former because she felt this was 'where I am at my best'. At this point she agreed to try a focus group as a means of testing potential customers' reaction to her paintings.

Wine, cheese, coffee and croissants were provided at a lively and relaxed meeting in the artist's studio. About half way through, during a break, the artist reported in exasperation that 'they all like the wrong pictures!'. A dozen examples of her work had been numbered and displayed and, to her horror, nearly all the participants preferred the landscapes over her favourite abstracts!

She soon realized that her customers' reaction should guide her actions and to this day her home remains festooned with the unwanted – yet much loved – abstract work while her landscapes grace the walls of her many paying customers. The focus group had proved a success and, among other things, demonstrated the dangers of being too emotionally involved with your product. Objectivity during the planning process is crucial!

BRAINSTORMING
Focus groups can be used to brainstorm ideas – perhaps for improvements to the product, for promotional methods or

even to find a suitable name for the new business. If you would like to do the latter, get the group to close their eyes and then clearly read out 12 pre-prepared words that illustrate the values of your business (for example, quality, friendly, cutting-edge, reliable...). Then get your group to open their eyes and write the first business names that come into their head. Note each person's ideas on a flip chart for all to see and to discuss. You will be amazed at both the enthusiasm and the results!

The focus group is just one of many research techniques that can be employed to increase your chances of success. You should leave nothing to chance as you embark on your journey into self-employment. After all, if you get it right, it could be the start of something big!

WHAT CONCLUSIONS SHOULD YOU DRAW?

'Looking before you leap' is essentially all to do with learning as much as you can about the 'marketing mix'. The marketing mix is about providing the right product or service, at the right price, at the right place, using the right promotion. So you need to use the findings from your research to decide on some key factors about your product:

- **Price** – how much will you will charge for your product, and will the market bear this price?

- **Positioning** – does your proposed product and price reflect your choice of market position? Are you going to go for quality (where you can charge premium rates) or quantity (where your lower prices will secure a high volume of sales)? Basically, are you going for high value or cheap and cheerful?

- **Location** – where are you going to base your business? Does this correspond with the geographical area you can profitably operate in?

You also need to decide on some more general points about your business. Your research should have informed you about all sorts of legal and financial points which you will need to cover. For example, you will need to think about:

- **Premises** – do you actually need a shop or an office premises? Is there a cheaper alternative way of housing your fledgling firm, at least until you have a clear appreciation of your prospects?

- **Form of business** – will you operate as a sole trader, in a partnership, as a limited company...? (see pages 15 and 16)

- **Costs** – how much will your business cost to set up? Do you need to borrow? How much?

- **Legalities** – what kind of insurance do you need? What will your health and safety policy be? Are there any professional standards to which you must adhere?

More information on these points is provided later in the chapter.

It's a lot to think about – setting up in business on your own is not always as easy as it might at first seem. But the more time you set aside to investigate anything that is going to enable you to be better prepared for what can be a challenging and an often uncertain future, the better – it will be time well spent and you won't regret it! And once you have collected information on all the points mentioned above, you are ready to draw up your business plan.

WRITING THE BUSINESS PLAN

Having gathered valuable information on your customers, competitors and suppliers you now need to do something with it – and this is where the business plan comes in. A business plan is a stand-alone document containing all the key information about your business – details of your skills, proposed activity, suppliers, market awareness, publicity plan and targets over the coming year.

WHAT IS A BUSINESS PLAN FOR?

A business plan is more than just a theoretical exercise – it is an excellent business tool that you avoid at your peril. It is a crucial representation of your objectives and the means by which you plan to achieve them, and it is a 'living' document that will require updating and revising as time passes. You can use it as:

- The core of the planning process before and after the day you actually start trading

- A map of the road you plan to take

- A way of measuring your actual progress against projected figures

- A touchstone to return to when you feel you have lost your way.

And last but by no means least, you can use it to get money! If you need funding in order to get things off the ground, you are going to need a business plan – it's as simple as that. Banks, business support agencies and other programmes will all need to assess the viability of your start-up, and to do this they need all the facts. They are unlikely to lend you money if you can't show how you are going to repay it – and if they are planning to *give* you money then they need to be confident that it will not go to waste. Remember, all organisations (and especially public services) need to account for their actions and your business plan will help them do this. Everything that is going to support your application for funding must be included to maximise your chances of receiving support.

The business plan is therefore a yardstick for external organisations to measure and record the ability and commitment of the entrepreneur and the potential success of the proposed business. It can also be used as a means of gaining access to training and ongoing support. It is therefore very important to be able to produce an accurate and detailed proposal if you're going to secure the help that you need to create a successful new business.

THE CONTENT

So we have identified what the business plan is for, but what about the content? A business plan usually contains the following sections, each of which is covered in more detail in the pages that follow:

- **Title page**

- **Contents page** (subsequent pages should be numbered)

- **CV** – brief overview of past employment and current skills

- **Business proposal** – outline of the product or service the business will provide

- **Objectives** – short, medium and long-term goals

- **SWOT analysis** – overview of the strengths, weaknesses, opportunities and threats relating to the proposed business

- **Market research** – summary of research carried out with competitors, suppliers and customers

- **Marketing** – including pricing plan and promotional strategy

- **Legalities** – including details of insurance requirements, health and safety issues, premises, business status and other contractual issues peculiar to the chosen business

- **Financial** – including survival budget, profit and loss account, balance sheet, sales forecast and cash flow forecast

- **Appendix** – to include all related text not vital to the plan content.

The business plan is written in report format. It is worth taking trouble over presentation, as you may be competing with other equally worthy applicants for limited funds. Take the advice of one aspiring business person who has been through the funding process: 'It would be wise not to forget the importance of accuracy, so make sure that you double check the figures and get someone to proofread the text.' You could ask a family or friend to do this.

The finished document must of course be tailored to your own goals and needs and the required format of the recipient. It would be wise to seek further advice to clarify any areas of doubt and get a second opinion on the suitability of this plan outline, before you take the matter any further. Let's look at the business plan in more detail.

CV (CURRICULUM VITAE)

The first page of your business plan should introduce yourself via a brief CV, so that the reader can quickly understand what sort of person they are going to be dealing with. This should contain information regarding your working history, skills and any previous experience relevant to your new business, whether it be business experience and/or training which will assist you in running the proposed business. A CV is required for each partner within a partnership.

BUSINESS PROPOSAL

This is a summary of your business idea. Describe the product/service you are offering, who your customers will be and why you believe they should buy from you rather than any competitors (your unique selling point – USP).

OBJECTIVES

You need to provide detailed information on your business and personal objectives for the first year, but you also need to give an indication of how you think the business will develop in subsequent years, looking as far ahead as you reasonably can.

SWOT ANALYSIS

As outlined earlier, a SWOT analysis is a study of the strengths, weaknesses, opportunities and threats relating to your business. You should present them in order of importance. Don't be afraid to include weaknesses and threats – they will show potential investors that you have thought through the situation and won't be taken unawares by unexpected problems, and you never know, investors or advisers might be able to offer help. Where possible, explain how you plan to compensate for or overcome weaknesses and threats.

MARKET RESEARCH

This section is used to summarise the research you have carried out (eg questionnaires, focus groups, product sampling) into customers, competitors and suppliers, and outline the conclusions of your investigations. Findings should be presented in a user-friendly graphic format (eg bar charts, pie charts etc) and you should show

how these underpin your proposal and inform your pricing policy and market positioning (see below). You should organise information under the following headings.

THE MARKETPLACE

You should describe your chosen marketplace, its size and present state. You should also provide a profile of your customer.

RESEARCH

Researching the marketplace is essential to any new business and you therefore need to provide evidence that proves you know that people want to buy your product or service. (See earlier in the chapter for detailed information on how to carry out research.) You need to show that the business will attract enough customers for you to be a success.

One owner/manager of a manufacturing business offers the following sound advice: 'Give an in-depth report on all the research that you have undertaken, in whatever form, giving numbers and types of potential customers contacted, the methods you have used, the results obtained and your conclusions. This research should demonstrate the basis on which you feel this business is going to succeed. Include any copies of questionnaires used, sources of information you have referred to and any correspondence that can support your evidence.'

COMPETITION

Provide details of any competition you may encounter, including the number of competitors, where they are based and explain how you will match that competition. Do a SWOT analysis on each competitor.

MACHINERY AND EQUIPMENT

Provide details and value of any equipment you already have and of any equipment you plan to purchase in order to start your business. These prices will need to be included in your start-up costs.

SUPPLIERS

It is most important to check out quality, price, convenience and availability of your intended suppliers before deciding who to use. Having only one supplier is something to be avoided as it means they could dictate terms from a position of strength. Explain which suppliers you plan to use and why you have chosen them.

MARKETING

Having proved in the previous section that there is a market for your product or service, you now need to show how you are going to let them know about it. This is a combination of your pricing strategy, your promotional plan and, of course, your ability to distribute and sell your product.

DISTRIBUTION AND SELLING

Explain who is going to sell your product or service and where and how it is going to be sold. Options to consider might include:

- Shop

- Craft fairs

- Local markets

- Mail order

- Wholesalers and distributors

- The internet

- Party plan

- Mobile service

- Personal selling.

If you are selling a service then your options might be different. Your market research should have given you a good idea of which mode of sale will be most appropriate – make sure you give evidence from this to back up your choice.

PRICING

You need to say how much you will be charging for your product or service, and use your research to show that your product/service is saleable at that price. Where possible, include a price list and show how your prices compare with those of your competitors.

ADVERTISING AND PROMOTION

This section should be used to outline how your product/service will be advertised and how much this will cost (particularly at the early stages of the start-up). The range of advertising and marketing options available to you is enormous – from a TV advertising campaign to a card in the window of your local newsagents. It's such a huge topic that this book dedicates a whole chapter to it – see page 46 for more information. However, for the purposes of the business plan, the usual rules apply – try to relate what you have found in your research to the promotional strategy you plan to use, and give as much detail as possible.

LEGALITIES

There is a growing list of red tape to deal with and you must demonstrate that you are aware of what you must do to abide by the rules and regulations. You'll need to cover the following points, and also think about each of the issues raised in the box on pages 42–44.

INSURANCE

List each of the different insurances that you will need (see page 17 for more details). For example, you will probably need public liability insurance and perhaps even product liability insurance or professional indemnity insurance. You should speak to an insurance broker and obtain recommendations and quotations. Don't forget that if you are going to use your car for business purposes you will need 'business use' insurance cover.

LICENCES AND OTHER STANDARDS

There are many businesses that require licences – for example, childminders, tobacco and alcohol sales, financial advisers, market stallholders, riding stables and so on. You must find out whether or not you require a licence for your business and provide that information. You may also find that you need to be a member of or affiliated to a professional association, in order to offer a quality assurance to customers. The local council adviser or relevant trade association will be able to help.

HEALTH AND SAFETY

Health and safety legislation protects the health and safety of the general public, employers, self-employed and employees. The regulations are extensive and you must ensure that you are aware of your responsibilities in this area, and outline them in your business plan. Check with your local Health and Safety Executive office or visit www.hse.gov.uk and include the relevant findings in this section.

TERMS AND CONDITIONS OF PAYMENT

This paperwork lays out what you are providing for your customer, so you need to include your terms and condition of payment. This includes information like:

- Whether all amounts will be payable at point of sale (eg in a shop)

- Whether or not you plan to take a deposit from customers

- Whether or not any deposit is refundable

- What happens if a customer/client withdraws before the contract is completed

- When outstanding balances will be due.

CONTRACTS

If the sale of your product or service requires a contract you may wish to include an example in your business plan.

PREMISES/PLANNING PERMISSION

You need to provide information on where your business will be based. If you run the business from home you probably won't need planning permission, but you will need to check on this and you must inform your insurance and mortgage companies of your intentions. If you are in rented accommodation, you may need a landlord's permission.

If you are operating from commercial premises you must ensure they have planning consent for your type of business; provide details on the size, location, rent, related costs and whether the premises are leasehold, easy in easy out etc (this is covered in more detail on pages 94–95)

FORM OF BUSINESS

Will you be a sole trader, in partnership, a limited company or a co-operative?

LEGALITIES CHECKLIST

Here is a checklist of the things you need to do to make sure your business is above board, together with some key facts on each point.

☐ **Inform the Tax Office**

● You need to do this within three months of trading start – or you could be fined £100

● The telephone number is 08459 154515

● You pay tax on the net profit your business makes – this is the actual profit you make *after* working expenses have been paid

● Your 'Personal Allowance' (what you can earn Tax Free) is £4895 per year (figure correct as at April 2006)

☐ **Register for NIC (National Insurance Contributions)**

● You register with the Contributions Agency via the Tax Office

● Self-employed NIC Class 2 is £2.10 per week for earnings over £4000

● Class 4 NIC is payable on profit of between £4895 and £32,760 per year

● Class 4 NIC stands at 8% on the difference between the upper and lower limits

☐ **Check for VAT liability**

● The current VAT threshold is £61,000

● This is based on *turnover* (the total amount of money your company takes, before any costs have been deducted) rather than profit

● This turnover figure is in a rolling 12 month period

● You can voluntarily register

● Contact Customs & Excise for an information pack – tel: 0845 010 9000

☐ **Check planning permission**

● Do not assume!

● Check with your Local Council Planning Department to see whether you need planning permission on business premises

● Check with landlord, council or building society for any restrictions on property use

☐ **Get the right insurances**

● Legal – motor vehicle and employers liability

● Public liability/product liability/professional indemnity

● Accident and/or sickness

● Goods in transit etc

☐ **Licences**

● Do you need one to operate? For example, credit licence, data protection, public performance ...

☐ **Health and safety**

● Do you need to complete a risk assessment on working activities?

● Check with the Health and Safety Executive (HSE) on regulations for your business – www.hse.gov.uk

● If you have five or more employees you must have a health and safety policy

☐ **Legal status**

● See pages 15–16 for more information

FINANCIAL SECTION

In this section you need to cover your budget and start-up costs, as well as including information such as a profit and loss account, balance sheet, sales forecast and cash flow forecast. You should discuss these subjects with an adviser on a one-to-one basis.

BUDGET

If this business is to provide all or most of your income, you must calculate your annual financial requirements and from this figure calculate your monthly drawings, or what you hope to take from the business for personal expenditure.

START-UP COSTS

Before you open your doors for business you need to calculate how much is needed to give your business the best chance of success. List all the equipment and supplies needed and their costs and any expenses incurred before the business starts. Give a brief description of these items and why they are needed, and outline how you plan to find them. Do not include items already owned or expenses already incurred.

FORECASTS

You will need to forecast your sales turnover as you expect it to be in the first year and you should then enter these figures into a monthly cash flow forecast which details your expenditure and income.

A profit and loss statement (which illustrates the business's potential profitability – or otherwise) can also be included at this stage. If you need to know more about sales forecasts, cash flow forecasts and profit and loss statements, ask your adviser.

FASCINATING FACTS

In the UK overall, 9% of the average gross weekly household income comes from self-employment. The proportion varies throughout the UK, with the highest (14%) in London, and the lowest (4%) in the North-East.
Source: Office for National Statistics, 1999–2002 (latest available figures)

CONCLUSION

This chapter has only given a brief overview of the business plan and market research processes. A great deal of reading and advice is available on this subject and a trip to your local bookshop, library or Enterprise Agency will give you an idea of the many and varied plan templates that you can choose from. You may also find it useful to look at the sample business plan provided in the appendix at the end of this book.

CHAPTER 3

Promoting your business

So you still want to be self-employed? You've read about the subject, you've researched your product or service and are confident that your price is right and that there is a viable marketplace for your business. You've taken proper legal, financial and business planning advice and written a decent business plan, which may have enabled you to acquire funding to get the business started. You may even have taken time out to get some training and are confident in the knowledge that you have done all you can to ensure that this venture is a success. You're raring to go. What happens next?

Well, the first (and absolutely crucial) thing you need to do is to communicate to your customers that your service or product is available – otherwise how will they know about it? If you don't promote your business effectively, you risk stopping it before it has even started; many aspiring entrepreneurs give little or no thought as to where their customers are going to come from, which can cost money and time. This chapter will look at a number of different ways of promoting and marketing your product or service and focus in detail on those that are most relevant to a small business start-up.

WHAT ARE THE OPTIONS?

The range of promotional methods available is huge – the sky is quite literally the limit: you could fly an aeroplane banner along a crowded summer's beach in Spain – you could stand in the rain outside a tube station with a sandwich board around your neck. Either will have benefits to your business and may well meet with some success. The checklist below is not exhaustive but it should give you a few ideas about how you could promote your new business. Here is a list of just some of the things you could do:

- Advertise in newspapers (national or local, including free press)

- Advertise on radio and TV

- Advertise in brochures, magazines and trade journals

- Get editorial coverage in any of the above by distributing press releases

- Advertise in catalogues and business directories (such as *Yellow Pages* and the *Thomson Directory*)

- Advertise in shop windows

- Advertise on posters, billboards, sandwich boards and your own vans

- Advertise on aeroplane banners

- Use e-marketing – via your own website or advertising on other people's websites

- Distribute leaflets through doors in areas where you think there may be potential customers (know as a 'leaflet drop')

- Send out direct mail marketing (eg mailshots/personal letters – either by post or via the internet)

- Use letter-headed stationery

- Organise a direct sales campaign

- Attend/exhibit at trade fairs

- Organise your own promotional event

- Give promotional talks

- Arrange a promotional stunt

- Sponsor an event or product

- Organise a competition

- Offer promotional gifts (known as merchandising)

- Offer discounts, special offers and bargains – eg 'buy one get one free' offers (know in the trade as 'BOGOFs') and loss leaders (which draw the customers in to buy, although they make a loss)

- Work with other businesses to help each other – known as 'partnership marketing'

- Create referrers ('centres of influence' – see below)

- Network and gain contacts and recommendations by word of mouth.

HOW TO CHOOSE?

Given the range of options, this may seem a little bewildering. However, the important thing is to work out which methods are best-suited to your business. With luck your market research will have revealed who your likely customers will be – and this should help you narrow down the list. For example, advertising in the local press when you are setting up an internet business selling throughout the country would not be a very wise move. In addition, financial limitations will probably rule out some of the more expensive options such as TV or billboard advertising.

So decisions about where to advertise will probably be relatively easy – your budget and the nature of your product or service will dictate the kinds of publications or websites in which you advertise. However, advertising alone is unlikely to be enough. As you will see in Chapter 4, keeping customers is of paramount importance – but in reality some are going to drift away and you'll need to develop an ongoing promotional strategy to attract new ones.

The paragraphs below therefore investigate some of the cheaper ways of getting your message across to your customers: direct sales, referral farms, press releases and events.

DIRECT SALES

A sympathetically and properly handled direct sales campaign could become an effective part of your promotional activity. It can be a most efficient method of getting your new message across to commercial customers and you may find that it paves the way to success.

Direct selling is not popular with new entrepreneurs because people generally don't like getting cold calls at home, and the thought of actually being the person making the calls seems even worse. However, it doesn't have to be like that. If you follow a few simple rules and take a structured approach with five simple steps (see below), direct sales can bring in happy customers quickly and profitably.

Remember, it is wise to treat your potential customers with the respect and courtesy that you would expect yourself, so do some research and observe some rules such as calling during business hours not weekends. If in doubt about anything ask your local Enterprise Agency or Business Link for advice before you get started.

THE DATA PROTECTION ACT AND TPS
Any one who records or processes information about their customers electronically or on paper has certain obligations under the Data Protection Act.

It is now a also legal obligation for anyone making direct marketing calls (or faxes) to ensure that they do not call individuals who have registered their wish not to be called with the Telephone (or fax) Preference Service (TPS).

Further information on the Data Protection Act and the TPS is available from the organisations listed in the Resources section at the end of this book.

THE FIVE-STEP FORMAT TO DIRECT SALES SUCCESS

The diagram below shows the five simple steps you need to follow to carry out an effective direct sales campaign. Each step is examined in more detail in the paragraphs that follow.

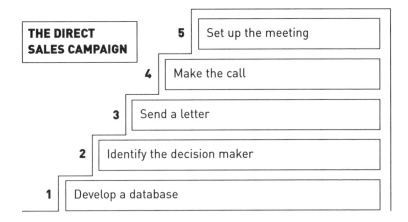

THE DIRECT SALES CAMPAIGN

5 Set up the meeting
4 Make the call
3 Send a letter
2 Identify the decision maker
1 Develop a database

1. DEVELOP A DATABASE

Start collecting details of prospective customers (referred to as 'prospects') on an action plan, under headings such as:

- Company name

- Address

- Telephone number

- Fax

- E-mail

- Notes.

Ideally you should collect this information in a spreadsheet or database.

2. IDENTIFY THE DECISION-MAKER
The first stage of the campaign involves simply calling the prospects to identify who will be able to make the decision to do business with you. Write the name down under a new heading, 'Decision maker'.

One painter and decorator entrepreneur describes how he approached this stage: 'I simply asked who arranged their property maintenance contracts. I didn't get bogged down with details – I just said I wanted to drop the person responsible for making these decisions a line first. As long as I was polite and to the point they were quite happy.'

3. SEND A LETTER
The next stage is to send a 'mail shot'. To do this, write a short introductory letter to each decision maker. Address them by name and explain who you are, what you do and that you may call them over the next fortnight. Remember to follow the 'KISS' rule – **k**eep **it s**hort and **s**imple. Leaflets can be added when the mail shot is posted. If you have your contact details in a database or spreadsheet you should be able to use a 'mail merge' to insert names and contact details more easily.

4. MAKE THE CALL
The moment has arrived! Once you've sent your introductory letter and allowed time for the postal service to deliver it to your prospect's desk, it's time to make that dreaded sales call. The

purpose of most calls is to fix a one-to-one appointment with your prospect to enable you to attempt to secure a commitment to buy. It would be wise to avoid becoming embroiled in detail on the phone.

Start the call by introducing yourself, your business and why you have called, then mention your letter (which they should remember) and eventually move on to suggest an appointment at a mutually convenient time. If they say 'no', don't panic! Ask them if they would like some more information and ask them whether you can make a note to call them again in six months, when they may have more time.

You should keep a record of your conversation under columns, headed 'notes' and 'action', so that you can diarise future appointments and recall times. Whatever the response, take notes on things discussed that are worth remembering ('I prefer to be called Jonnie' or 'I'm Sales Manager' or 'I can't see you for a month because I'm getting married' and so on). Showing that you remember these pieces of information can be crucial in building up a rapport with your clients.

You may find that you are alarmingly reluctant to pick up the phone; another cup of coffee may suddenly become vital to the day's success. Beware! This is your mind indulging in diversionary tactics. You must avoid distractions if you are going to be able to build up a rhythm and hit your call target. You will find that if you focus, things will get easier, and you will relax into the routine and develop a sense of rhythm. The box below gives a few key tips to help you on your way.

TOP TIPS FOR DIRECT SALES CALLS

- Get organised and focused

- Have a trial run

- Clear your desk

- Avoid interruptions

- Don't get sidetracked or try to do something else at the same time

- Have a script and technical data/price lists handy for reference purposes or in case your mind goes blank

- Some people like to have relaxing instrumental music playing in the background to keep them calm

- Above all, try to relax and don't forget to smile – people can tell if you are tense!

5. SET UP THE MEETING

If your client is interested, arrange a mutually convenient time to meet them – and congratulations! You may find that you now need to brush up on your negotiating skills... so read on.

NEGOTIATION – TWO EARS, ONE MOUTH!

Like making that first direct sales call, meeting a prospect to sell them your product or service and negotiate terms can be an intimidating prospect. The key point is that to negotiate successfully, it is first necessary to understand the customer's need. This is achieved through listening, rather than talking – remember that you have two ears and one mouth, and you should use them in that proportion!

REAL-LIFE STORY

A window cleaner was once asked to make a 'pitch' for cleaning the windows of an enormous office block. It was a huge job! Great news! Or was it? He had no problems with the job itself. What troubled him was the negotiation process, so much so that he had even thought about cancelling the meeting. What gave him the confidence to go and secure the business was something called the five-step format. More details on this are given below.

THE FIVE-STEP FORMAT TO NEGOTIATION SUCCESS

This is a structured approach to meeting the challenge of negotiating that big deal that will make all the difference to your business. It comes in the form of five simple steps that can help you plan and control what can be a nerve-racking occasion. The diagram below shows the different steps of the process, each of which is examined in more depth in the paragraphs that follow.

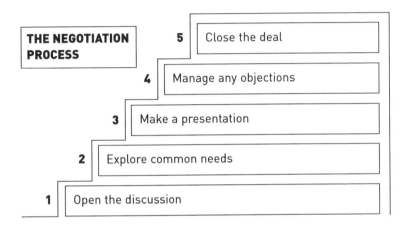

THE NEGOTIATION PROCESS

5 Close the deal

4 Manage any objections

3 Make a presentation

2 Explore common needs

1 Open the discussion

1. OPEN THE DISCUSSION

Preparation and first impressions are crucial. You must do your homework *and* be ready to stride confidently across the room, look your prospective customer in the eye and greet them with a smile and a firm handshake. Make some appropriate small talk as you get settled, then clearly and politely explain what you perceive to be the objectives of the meeting and invite them to agree.

2. EXPLORE COMMON NEEDS

If you are nervous, it is very easy to talk too much – and when you are negotiating for a big deal it is the last thing you should do. Instead, you should explore your customer's needs by listening to what they have to say. Don't persuade – ask open questions, listen to the response, and take notes. When you understand what they want you can tailor your presentation in order to get the business.

3. MAKE A PRESENTATION

It is always advisable to have something to show the potential customer; often this comes in form of a portfolio that illustrates the finer points of your product or service. When presenting your portfolio you must:

- Focus on your customer's needs

- Outline how they relate to the relevant features of your product or service

- Explain the benefits to the client of doing business with you.

If you use your prepared portfolio in conjunction with the list of their wishes that you made during the earlier phase of your conversation, you will appear professional and sympathetic to their needs. They will feel that you have been listening to them and that may be a novel experience!

4. MANAGE ANY OBJECTIONS

Any concerns or objections the prospective customer raises should be embraced as a positive development – they show that that you have got their attention and they are engaging with your product, and once they are dealt with you are closer to doing business with your customer. Once again the first thing you should do is to listen to what your customers say. Ask questions to clarify the point they are trying to make and produce realistic answers to the issues raised that demonstrate you have been listening. Don't forget to make notes.

5. CLOSE THE DEAL

Many people conduct themselves admirably in the sales scenario. They do everything right – they listen, make a good presentation, even deal with objections, but then fail to ask for the order! Don't be shy – the customer is there because they are interested in your product so you have every right to ask them if they would like to make an order. Negotiation should be a natural process leading to a point where both parties are ready to do business. Business is done when you gain commitment from the customer and this only ever happens when the customer decides.

PRESS RELEASES

WHAT IS A PRESS RELEASE, AND WHO IS IT FOR?

The business information company Cobweb describes a press release as being 'a simplified story about your business or a particular aspect of it, written from a news point of view'. Press releases are written when you have a newsworthy subject to write about, such as the launch of a new product, a change of image or a forthcoming event. You produce a document describing the chosen subject and send it to the chosen media company in the hope that the editor or journalist will use it as the basis for an article or programme. This achieves two things – you get your publicity and the media company gets a story to tell. As you can see this is a mutually beneficial arrangement.

Regional, free, trade and national press all receive and use press releases, as do trade journals and some websites. Your local and national radio and television companies might also be interested in your story. Publications such as *BRAD*, *Benn's Media Directory* and *Willings Press Guide* will help you identify magazines, papers and journals that may be appropriate for your business – you should be able to find copies at your local library.

The press release is one of the few free promotional methods available. With a little practice and advice you may find that writing press releases that are imaginative, interesting and eye-catching could become one of your regular promotional activities. This will broaden the appeal of your business and reach out to new customers, which will in turn help you make bigger and better profits.

HOW TO WRITE A PRESS RELEASE

The first stage to writing a press release is – you guessed it – research. Make some phone calls to find out who to send your press release to – you are looking for writers, editors and journalists who have access to the kind of publication you want your business promoted in. Talk to the journalists or editors to find out:

- What format they would like to receive your press release in – email, hard copy or fax

- What sort of material they are looking for

- Whether any future publications are going focus on a particular theme – especially one which is relevant to your business. For example, if you run a hotel and the newspaper you contacted is planning a leisure and tourism theme in two months' time, then you are more likely to get your press release accepted and get the copy into that than the current edition.

Remember, journalists and editors are busy people and if you get the timing, format and theme right you will have a better chance of success. The box on page 58 gives some top tips on how to make sure your press release is interesting, engaging and likely to result in good publicity. But first, here are some points on the standard structure and presentation you should follow:

- **Label** – write 'NEWS RELEASE' or 'PRESS RELEASE' clearly at the top of the page

- **Headline** – give each press release a headline. This should be a concise statement of its content – it's not necessary for it to be witty because the journalist will probably want to invent a title of their own

- **Embargo** – use this only if you absolutely have to. An embargo is when you state that information in the press release cannot be published until a certain date

- **Paper** – use letter-headed paper or put your name address and contact details at the end

- **Presentation** – double space your text so that the recipient can edit it

- **End** – When you come to the end write 'end'. If you need to use a second page write 'continued' at the foot of the page.

TOP TIPS ON PRESS RELEASES

Timing – you might increase your chances of success if you get the timing right and ensure that your press release coincides with a popular topic or a current issue of the day

Newsworthiness – remember, your press release needs to contain new, interesting information that editors are going to feel their readers will want to know. Examples of newsworthy press releases include those concentrating on a campaign, anniversary, competition, controversial opinion or topical subject

KISS – keep it short and simple, using one side of A4 where possible and restricting the text to three main points

Objectivity – a press release should be written from an objective point of view. If you need to include personal opinions, use quotations

Quotations – use these to enliven the message and to express personal opinions

Novelty – you will achieve more success with press releases if you write about something that is unusual or eye-catching

The human touch – try to focus on the human story because people like reading about other people and what they are up to. If you have something to offer the reader, you could try addressing them directly (eg 'would you like to win...?').

Jargon – avoid this. Don't use flowery language and don't be too technical

Photos – these are a useful addition to a press release, especially if they are relevant and have a caption that relates to part of the text. Above all the photograph must be of good quality – at least 300dpi at print size if you are sending them electronically

Notes for editors – you can include details that may be of use to the editor such as names of individuals, time and place of photo opportunities and brief descriptions of organisations and events under the heading 'notes for editors' at the end of the press release. This avoids clogging up the text of your press release with unwanted detail and ensures that the recipient has all the information they are going to need

Accuracy – make sure you get someone to proofread your text.

WHAT HAPPENS AFTER THE PRESS RELEASE HAS BEEN SENT?

Once you have done your research, written your press release and sent it off, you might like to make sure that it has been received and check to see if the journalist needs any more information. You must be available to talk to journalists and even be prepared for interviews.

Remember, all journalists work to a deadline and need prompt responses if they are to get their job done. They will appreciate someone who is helpful and keeps their promises. You would be well-advised to keep in contact with them, because they will always need a reliable source and may be able to help you again at some point in the future. If you can develop a good relationship with them you may find that your business is mentioned positively in more than just one article.

EVENTS

Your promotional strategy should be diverse and, above all, imaginative if you are to succeed and build a profitable new start-up business. An essential ingredient in your marketing campaign could be setting up and running your own event or attending an event or exhibition run by someone else. Bearing in mind the budget limitations you may be under, the latter may be your best option.

The range of events is very broad – from craft fairs or county shows to specialist trade fairs and big national shows like the NEC retail exhibition – so there's bound to be something that will get you in front of your prospective customers. And if you can't afford a stand at someone else's show, why not go anyway to walk the floor meeting and greeting? There's no law against it! Events are nearly always harder work than you imagined but they often bring rewards unobtainable elsewhere and you can always relax when it's all over!

WHAT WILL AN EVENT DO FOR YOUR BUSINESS?

There are many reasons to get involved in events – no matter how big or small they are and whether you are the organiser, an exhibitor or just an attendee. Here are a few of them:

- **Direct sales** – depending on the event you attend and the nature of the product you are selling, you may be able to make sales there and then, so be prepared to 'talk the talk'

- **Networking** – events can be great networking tools, opening doors to new customers and contacts that you would never otherwise have met. Similarly it can be a great way of using contacts you already have to spread the word. One entrepreneur reported: 'I set up my first stall at a craft fair and within an hour had met any number of people who knew me. They asked me all about my business, and then went home, told family and friends, the word got around in no time'

- **Research** – you have the opportunity to meet customers, competitors and suppliers, many of whom will be valuable sources of information – so an event can be a just the right occasion to conduct research into your marketplace

- **Inspiration** – this could be just around the corner so keep an eye open for new products, services and sales methods; it's essential to keep up to date and to be open to new ideas.

THE PRACTICALITIES

An event is an investment and, as such, must bring in a financial return. Careful planning is called for to ensure that maximum value is extracted from the time, effort and money you put in. Your probable objectives are to increase sales, to network and to maximise the PR (public relations) potential of the event so you need to make sure that everything you do pushes your 'message' and that you come across as well-organised and professional.

The checklist below includes points that should be relevant whether you are attending someone else's event, displaying a stand or organising your own event.

EVENT CHECKLIST
Advance planning

☐ **PR** – send a press release, contact journalists and stir it up!

☐ **Invitations** – send them (RSVP) out in good time and monitor the replies to make sure the numbers are right. If you are exhibiting at someone else's event, why not invite a journalist to visit you at your stand?

☐ **Name cards** – are you going to have them for your guests?

☐ **Food** – if you need it make sure you have a reliable good quality source

☐ **Seating** – plan this carefully – is there enough space for everybody?

☐ **Photographer** – have you arranged to have photographs taken? These could be useful in future promotional material

☐ **The venue** – check it out; you don't want unpleasant surprises!

☐ **Directions** – do your guests need them?

☐ **Parking** – is it adequate?

☐ **Exhibition stand** – will it compare favourably with the competition? Who is next door? Will they overshadow you? Check: if so, try to change site

---

☐ **Design and presentation** – make sure there is consistency throughout your products (logo, strap line, stand banner, t-shirts, posters etc)

☐ **Proofread** – everything

☐ **Clothing** – buy some polo shirts and get them embroidered with company ID if possible, or at least dress smartly and make sure everybody is wearing a badge with your organisation's name and logo

☐ **Equipment** – is it going to work? What happens if it fails? For example, do you have OHPs if the PowerPoint projector fails?

☐ **Insurance** – have you taken out the necessary insurances?

☐ **Promotions** – consider making an offer exclusive to the show available for visitors (eg 10% off)

☐ **More promotions** – have a business card draw with a prize and the use the cards as the basis for a mail shot.

WHAT TO TAKE

☐ **Portfolio/samples** – prepare a portfolio or sample (depending on your product) for demonstration purposes. Have order forms at the ready

☐ **Stock** – if you are selling your product, will you have enough stock?

☐ **Stationery** – have you enough cards, leaflets, brochures and order forms for the event?

☐ **First aid kit** – remember to bring one.

ON THE DAY

☐ **Back at base** – remember to leave your answerphone on back at the office or have calls diverted to your mobile in case people need to contact you

☐ **Communication** – have a brief meeting at the beginning of the event to ensure everybody is 'on message' and clear about procedure

☐ **Diary** – have this available to arrange meetings with contacts and potential customers

☐ **Records of attendees should be kept**

☐ **VIPs** – look after them

☐ **Networking** – if you have the opportunity, visit other exhibitors and network to try to gain useful contacts and possibly even develop a 'referral farm' (see below)

☐ **Evaluation** – how did it go? What could you do better next time? Did it help make your business more profitable? Are you getting more clients/customers as a result of your event? If so – do it again! If not, think carefully about what you could have done better and make notes so that you get more out of future events

☐ **Wow!** – you can relax after the show!

THE REFERRAL FARM

It is well worth having a go at creating a referral farm for your business, because once established they will become a major asset to your company. You may find that they contribute substantially to your profitability and, apart from a little imagination and effort, they won't have cost you a penny. In a business world of spiraling fuel prices and ever higher business rates, that's something worth knowing about. But what on earth is a 'referral farm'?

INTRODUCING REFERRAL FARMS

'This new restaurant is a cracker. Great meal, good service too, you ought to go there for that dinner you've got to organise.' This is the kind of comment a restaurateur would love to hear. Wouldn't it be nice if someone somewhere was praising your business like this? Business referrals are like gold dust and you want as many of them as you can get. Happy customers who are well satisfied with your product or service will tell others about the experience. Think about it. Have you ever had a good meal at a restaurant? How many people did you talk to about it?

A 'referral farm' is essentially a satisfied customer or a business associate who values the service you provide, and who tells other people about your product, which leads directly to an increase customers for your business. One employer elaborated: 'The good manager is someone who creates profits through other people. Equally, a good business person will find ways of creating customers through other people, or through what I choose to call "referral farms". Referral farms are places where people understand your business, appreciate its strengths and will happily recommend your business over and over again.'

Referral farms come in many shapes and sizes – the only limit is your imagination. The box below gives a few examples.

REAL-LIFE REFERRAL FARMS

A football club

A builder created a referral farm out of a local football club sponsorship deal. He bought a big silver cup, a new set of kit and paid for the club's excellent social event each year. As a consequence he built more conservatories, loft conversions and house extensions for footballers and their friends and relations than anyone else.

Marina and caravan park owners

A gas appliance repair and maintenance businessman visited the managers and owners of marinas and caravan parks where there were plenty of gas appliances that needed constant maintenance, safety checks and repair work. He

---

talked enthusiastically about his business and listened to the manager's needs, helping where he could. This direct approach enabled him to secure support. When the first referrals came in he worked hard to establish a reputation for providing an efficient and reliable service at a reasonable cost. Not surprisingly, every time a yacht or caravan owner wanted help the staff recommended his service. Business boomed.

A gardening programme

A landscape gardener made a referral farm out a radio gardening programme. He made a regular contribution to the programme and as a result he began to be invited to give talks at events. He began to be recommended by radio listeners and those to whom he gave talks as an expert and the word soon got round. This is his advice: 'Be a specialist – it was the best thing that happened to my business! My reputation was enhanced and this "media referral farm" started to produce enquiry after enquiry.'

CREATING REFERRAL FARMS

The best way to get referrals is to go out and look for referral farms. Start the process off by collecting details of potential referral farms on an action plan under headings such as company name, address, telephone number, fax, E-mail and so on. Then send a letter to introduce yourself and follow the directions in the section earlier in this chapter covering direct sales.

If you succeed in arranging a meeting with them, make sure you focus on the benefits of your product or services to their customers. For example, in the 'Marina and caravan park' example above, the key selling point was a fast, efficient service and a problem-free holiday with well-maintained gas equipment. Try to keep it casual and don't forget to take leaflets, technical information and anything else that might be useful. Why not consider leaving a small poster with them as well?

When that first, precious customer is referred to you, you must pull out all the stops. Get the job done efficiently and promptly. The referrer will be watching and, if happy, will soon start recommending you on a regular basis – and hey presto, you have another referral farm! Thank your referral farm for their efforts and whenever possible recommend the referral farm's services to your clients – one good turn deserves another.

Of course, satisfied customers are natural referral farms. The next chapter will look in detail at how to keep your clients happy – resulting in benefits for everyone.

CHAPTER 4

Keeping customers

Having written your business plan, found the requisite funds and run a good promotional campaign, you should find the customers start to call. Now all you have to do is keep them happy – both to ensure that they return and use your product or service again, and to make sure they spread the word about your business.

But, like so many things, keeping customers is easier said than done. There will be some natural 'leakage' and even with the best of intentions and the most organised business possible, it is inevitable that you will get at least some complaints and disappointed customers. You will have to keep promoting your business to compensate for this – but there are ways of making sure you keep this 'leakage' to a minimum. This chapter will look firstly at ways of building a relationship with a customer through good customer service in order to make sure they return to you, and secondly at what happens when it all goes wrong and how to turn a complaining customer into a happy one.

CUSTOMER SERVICE

'I don't know where the next customer's going to come from! The initial surge of customers that occurred during the first nine months of my business has dwindled to a disconcerting level.' This is the story of one IT consultant – and it's not an unusual one.

Customers are the lifeblood of any business, and the best and easiest people to do business with are your existing customers: you know them, they know you, they like your product or service because they have already bought it and they may want to do business with you again. It is much less expensive to retain existing customers than to go out and find new ones every month. Dr Philip Kotler, a well known marketing commentator, estimated that 'the cost of attracting a new customer may be five times the cost of keeping a current customer happy'. So doing business with existing clients and making sure you keep them happy is pretty cost-effective.

Remember, happy customers may come back again and again and will recommend to others that they do the same. So if you manage the relationship that you have with your customer carefully, you'll reap the rewards in the form of repeat business and referrals whatever ever type of business you run. The art of managing customer relationships effectively and profitability is known as 'relationship marketing'.

RELATIONSHIP MARKETING
The Chartered Institute of Marketing (CIM) describes five different levels of customer relationship:

1. **Basic** – where the business person sells a product without any further contact with the customer (for example, buying a newspaper or a chocolate bar from your local newsagents)

2. **Reactive** – where the customers are encouraged to call the salesperson if there is a problem

3. **Accountable** – where the salesperson telephones the customer to see if there are any problems and to elicit ideas for future product or service improvements

4. **Proactive** – where the salesperson contacts the customer on a regular basis

5. **Relationship marketing** – where the salesperson and customer work together to ensure that all aspects of the deal suits the needs of both parties, not just for the present but for the future.

The development of a successful ongoing partnership (ie the fifth level) between the small-business owner and the customer is the essence of relationship marketing. It is defined as being 'the process of creating, building up and managing long-term relationships with customers, distributors and suppliers', so it goes beyond just selling. Here are some tips on building up the right kind of long-term relationship with your customers:

- **Customer care** – customers need to feel valued in order to be loyal and this can only be achieved by developing an excellent customer care policy

- **Business unity** – don't forget, everybody in your business must be convinced that this extra effort is going to be worth it. Everyone has to be 'on board'

- **Innovation** – you must seek to consistently improve your product and service to keep ahead of the competition. You must try to keep satisfying your customer's needs by being innovative

- **Communication** – Contact your customers frequently to keep them updated with developments. This could be via a newsletter, special offer, event or email. Make sure they perceive you as being interesting and excited about your business – because they will be too; its contagious!

- **Information** – build a database or some other means to record information about your customerss. This enables you to develop customer profiles to ensure that you can accurately target your goods and services.

Take a look at the real-life stories below to see how relationship marketing can be used to great effect, whatever the size of your company.

REAL-LIFE STORY
Tesco
You don't have to look far to find a big, profitable high-street name that values relationship marketing to the extent that it is a crucial element of their overall customer service approach. Tesco launched their loyalty card scheme to encourage customers to collect card points as they shop in the store.

The customer gets rewards points and saves money, and in return Tesco collects valuable customer information because each time the customer uses a card, their details are added to a purchase history. This is used to build customer profiles, which in turn enables the store to:

- Predict future buying behaviour and

- Improve their understanding of how they might be able to satisfy customer needs more effectively (and more profitability)

- Improve future advertising campaigns and customer communication.

IT entrepreneur
An IT entrepreneur set up a database to improve her customer communication. She created a newsletter which was sent out to everybody on a biannual basis. This newsletter commented upon the latest developments in technology and it contained special offers that were exclusive to the newsletter recipients. She also developed a website, which became an integral part of the way she communicated with clients, allowing them to use an online enquiry facility and to arrange to attend an event or enter a competition.

As a result of the relationship she built with her customers using these methods, she generated more interest in her business and a sense of belonging among her customers who, being more aware of what she had to offer, did more business with her. 'I managed to create a little community composed of everyone associated with my growing company', she says. 'These regular contacts brought an added value to the process of doing business. It also meant that my relationship with my customers improved, which meant that we did more business and I made more money!'

HANDLING COMPLAINTS

No matter how good your product and relationship marketing skills, you're never going to please everyone. Running a small business is almost always going to involve dealing directly with people – so when you get a dissatisfied customer it's going to be you who has to face up to the situation and deal with it, whether you like it or not. If you leave it unresolved, unhappy customers will tell family and friends about their grievances and this can damage your reputation – you could find yourself with a sort-of negative 'referral farm' (see previous chapter), which would be particularly damaging.

The small business can ill afford unhappy customers who won't forget that they were not treated well or that their feelings have been ignored, especially if they have gone to the trouble of making a complaint which has not been resolved to their satisfaction. This is sometimes especially true in rural areas, where there may be fewer potential customers and no way of hiding a bad service in 'the crowd'.

There are many reasons why complaints are not handled properly. For example, many businesses are ill-prepared for and taken aback by unhappy customers. In a small business every complaint may seem like a personal insult – after all, it may be you they are complaining about and there may be no one else but you to deal with it! This can be bad for morale.

As one property rental agent reports, his unhappy customer 'wasn't just annoyed, he was furious, and started banging his fist on my desk. It was really upsetting for me – I felt as if he was blaming me personally for everything that was wrong with the house he had rented from us'. It can be a stressful business dealing with someone who may be upset and angry, especially in the often-lonely and more personal world of self-employment. However, if you follow the rules given below, handling a complaint should be straightforward.

RULES FOR DEALING WITH A COMPLAINT

If you stick to a clear procedure to handle all complaints then you should find you have more confidence and you are able to take them less personally. Your customer will also feel that they are being listened to and, with luck, will go away feeling satisfied with the solution you have negotiated with them. So what do you have to do? Well, first of all, try remember how frustrated or cross you were last time you felt like making a complaint. Most customers are looking to hear three sentences in response to their comments: the first is 'I'm sorry', the second is 'don't worry' and the third is 'I'll sort it'. Keep this in mind as you work through the following steps.

1. LISTEN
The first thing to do is listen to your customer and acknowledge that they may have a grievance. This should calm the situation and help your customer feel that they are being taken seriously.

2. FIND A SUITABLE PLACE TO DISCUSS THINGS FURTHER
If the initial meeting takes place in public, you should find somewhere private so that you can discuss the matter away from other customers. There is only one thing worse than a complaint, and that is a public complaint.

3. ASK QUESTIONS
Now is the time to encourage the customer to fully explain their concerns so that they feel they have put their case as completely as possible. You don't want them to leave thinking 'I forgot to mention...' as this will mean that their complaint has not been fully addressed. Ask open-ended questions using words such as 'explain...', 'tell me...' 'what?' and 'how?'. Once you have pinpointed what lies behind the customer's concern you can seek to identify how the issue may be resolved to everyone's satisfaction – you are ready for the next stage.

4. NEGOTIATE
Dealing with a complaint is a negotiation process. Once the customer has fully elaborated on the reasons for their complaint,

both parties can enter into the negotiation process. This can only take place when the participants are both willing and prepared to be flexible. If your customer remains angry you have not got to the bottom of the problem and should return to the questioning phase to uncover hidden issues that still create a barrier to a satisfactory solution.

Of course, the solution you agree on must be acceptable to both parties – after all, there may be things you are *not* prepared to do. In fact, being open and frank about what you can and can't do will often bring a sense of reality to the proceedings and help the customer comprehend the parameters of the possible resolution.

HANDLING OBJECTIONS

If the customer raises concerns or objections about the proposed solution, use the following process:

- **Acknowledge** – indicate that you have taken on board their objection

- **Probe** – ask more questions to help you understand their reasons. It may be that they have additional concerns that they forgot to mention earlier in your conversation

- **Answer** – do your best to explain how you have taken on board their objections and, if necessary, suggest another compromise

- **Confirm** – see below.

---

5. CONFIRM

Once the solution has been agreed upon, you should confirm clearly what has been agreed. Get the customer to acknowledge that the proposed action will deal with their concerns. You could even make a note of what you have both decided to do to avoid any uncertainty.

Remember, it's not your job to eat humble pie when faced with a complaint, but it is your job to sympathetically negotiate a solution to the customer's problem. If you deal with a complaint effectively and professionally, you can actually turn it to your advantage. As the story below shows, a satisfied complainant will feel equally inclined to pass on positive views about your business.

REAL-LIFE STORY

'I went to see a film at a cinema complex and was disappointed to find that the only seats available were the very front ones, which I find very uncomfortable, so I decided to leave without seeing the film. On my way out I told the manager about the situation, but didn't expect him to do anything because I had been late arriving and it was my fault that there was little choice in where to sit. Imagine my surprise when I was not only given a refund of the cost of the tickets but was given free tickets to another film?'

Comment
This is an excellent example of how, if handled well, a complaint can be turned on its head to positive effect. The cinema-goer was pleasantly surprised at how their complaint had been dealt with and told many friends about it; disappointment was transformed into a positive public relations exercise that produced excellent feedback at little or no cost to the cinema.

CHAPTER 5

Successful staff

As your business becomes more and more successful and the customers starts to roll in, you may find that you no longer have capacity in your existing setup to deal with the extra work. You need help! Help in the form of employees. Employing people and delegating work carries with it a new set of challenges, which must be faced if you are to continue along the road towards success. This chapter will explore the relationship between you and your staff, starting with your first employee then moving on to looking at how to delegate and how to cope when your business starts to grow faster.

YOUR FIRST EMPLOYEE

Taking on your first employee can be a daunting process. There's plenty to think about, including:

- Job descriptions

- Job adverts

- Interviews

- Legislation

● Administration

● Tax

● National Insurance.

As ever, preparation is the key to success. This section will take you through the process of selecting and employing your first member of staff.

SKILLS AND JOB DESCRIPTION

One of the first things you should do is work out a job description, which provides an overview of the job's purpose, the salary being offered and the new recruit's duties, responsibilities, holidays and hours. Based on this, you should then prepare a person specification detailing the qualifications, experience, hours of availability and other requirements you expect of the person who will fill the role. This avoids confusion and gives you a good basis on which to asses the job candidates' skills and suitability.

JOB ADVERTS

You must choose carefully where you advertise the position. Options include:

● Newspapers – local and national

● Trade magazines

● Job Centre

● Card in shop window

● Internet – many paid ads in newspapers and magazines may include a free ad on the internet, but you may find specialist websites in your job area which will gain you access to the right audience.

You need to ensure that the medium you choose is appropriate and relevant to the job. Will your target audience read the newspaper you have chosen, for example?

Base the job advert on the job description and personal profile you have prepared. Make sure you remember to include details of how you would like applicants to apply. Ask them to send a CV and cover letter. Some larger employers prepare an application pack to send out, including an application form, which ensures that they get all the information they need from each candidate.

INTERVIEWS AND SELECTION

As one company director points out, CVs and covering letters give you 'a chance to make an initial selection on the basis of qualifications and the quality of correspondence and its content'. This enables you to filter out the less suitable applicants and focus your time more productively on interviewing your shortlisted candidates.

Plan how you would like to go about the interview process, and decide how you are going to conduct the interviews. It is always a good idea to have a checklist ready to ensure that you ask each candidate the same types of questions and cover all the relevant areas each time you interview someone. Allow yourself a gap between each interview to make notes on the candidate and reflect on what you think of them – it's amazing how easy it is to mix people up after you've seen a few!

The purpose of the interview is, of course, to check the suitability of the potential employee's skills, personality and compatibility. But the interview does not have to be the only thing you do during the selection process. Some small businesses like to provide some sort of test for prospective employees, while others may ask candidates to make a presentation. It all helps the decision-making process.

DISCRIMINATION

You are required by law not to discriminate and to ensure that your selection procedure is fair to everyone on the grounds of race, gender, disability and age. The Sex Discrimination Acts 1975 and 1986, the Equal Pay Amendments in 1996, the Race Relations Act 1976 (amended 2003), the Disability Discrimination Act 2005 and the Rehabilitation of Offenders Act 1974 (amended 2006) and the Employment Equality (Age) Regulations 2006, among others, lay down the law for

> recruitment. If in doubt, take advice from an enterprise agency or solicitor and ensure that your paperwork conforms to the law.

MAKING A JOB OFFER

An initial job offer will usually be made over the phone. Written confirmation, detailing the terms of employment, can follow by post. Your new employee is unlikely to hand in their notice until they have something in writing proving that you will offer them a job.

Don't forget the unsuccessful candidates; they may be waiting expectantly by the phone. Try to remember what it was like when you were job-hunting, and let them down gently. Remember how easy it is to develop negative PR.

LEGALITIES

You are required by law to have in place employer's liability insurance, so have a word with your local insurance brokers and compare prices.

If you have fewer than five employees, a pre-written health and safety policy is not obligatory. However, this quite complex matter must be explored carefully with an adviser. You might need to research risk assessments, first aid, rules governing the movement of hazardous substances, injuries and accident regulations, and the use of protective clothing. The Health and Safety Executive (0845 345 0055) is a good place to start.

You must contact your local tax office (0845 714 3143) to sort out PAYE and National Insurance for the new employee. These organisations will have checklists and guides to help you with your preparation. The *No-nonsense guide to government rules and regulations for setting up your business* is particularly useful, and is available by calling the DTI publications order line on 0845 015 0020 (reference URN 04/885).

LOOKING AFTER YOUR NEW EMPLOYEE

The first day at work can be a nerve-racking business, so it is always a good idea to put together an induction process to help your new employee get used to their new working environment. A smooth transition into their new role will be beneficial to both employee and employer, so it is a good idea to put a little thought into this. Make sure you cover:

- **Orientation** – where things are (everything from toilet and kettle to fax machine, files, pens or raw materials)

- **Job description** – exactly what the new employees responsibilities are, and how they do their job

- **Terms, conditions and prospects** – eg bonus payments, performance targets, career prospects, pay slips

- **Training** – find out any training needs they may have – prepare well and find out what courses are available locally.

LOOKING AFTER YOURSELF

There have been many small business owner-managers who abided by the rules and researched all the legal issues, but never gave a thought to the fact that their own role was undergoing a radical transformation – from sole trader to employer. This sometimes comes as quite a shock, and you must not leave yourself out of your considerations when planning the expansion of your business.

Good managers are always well prepared; they provide their employees with adequate access to information and give feedback through the appraisal process. You might want to consider getting some training yourself. Some useful websites are shown in the Resources section at the back of this book, and from these you can glean additional information on all the points mentioned in this chapter.

Expansion is often impossible without becoming an employer. Well-trained and motivated staff will eventually become one of the greatest assets your business possesses. So embrace the challenge as well the change and take that first step towards a bigger, better and more profitable business. However, in the words of a local garage owner: 'When you do anything in business, lad, make sure you go forward steady.'

DELEGATION

Picture the scene. It has been a hectic day – as usual. The phone has rung at least a dozen times, you've attended three meetings and you couldn't begin to count the pieces of paper you've handled. You've dealt with five queries from colleagues who unexpectedly arrived in your office, and there have been two major crises to sort out. You've been so busy – but you don't really feel you have achieved anything. There seems to be too much to do and just not enough time.

Does that sound familiar? One of the principal causes of business chaos such as this is the failure to delegate. Shortage of time, constant fire-fighting and a hectic office or workshop indicate that you're taking on too much. If you don't have any employees to help you, you need to think about taking some on or buying in help (for example a book-keeper). If you do have employees, then you need to learn to delegate! (You may also find the section on time management in the next chapter useful.)

Delegation has been described as 'doing things well through others'. It becomes an essential business tactic as your business begins to pick up pace because you will have less and less time to deal with the growing amount of paperwork that lands on your desk. In that sort of chaos, mistakes can happen, opportunities may be missed and customers can be unhappy – all resulting in bad publicity.

LEARNING TO DELEGATE

Sitting down with some friends, your partner or co-workers to work out what repetitive and uncomplicated tasks need to be dealt with on a regular basis, and by whom, during the working week. This will not only afford you a proper overview of your company's activity but it will help you prioritise its activity, and then to decide who is going to be responsible for what in the future.

For instance, you may find that you have been doing a couple of relatively mundane things every week, such as the post or VAT. You may be the person who goes to the bank every day, just because that's the way it has always been. With only a little thought, it is easy to see that your time would be better spent dealing with matters that are more productive and, most importantly, more profitable. Here's your chance. Talk to staff (if you already have them), partners and colleagues about getting someone else to deal with this relatively unproductive and repetitive work, so that you can concentrate on such areas as promoting your business better. You will be managing your business more effectively as a result.

Of course it is important, when delegating jobs to others, that you take care that they are on board and keen to participate in their new roles. Failure to do this can result in resentment and division. If possible, people should feel that the new way forward was, in part, suggested by them too. Everyone should feel that they are part of the process of change; the change will then be embraced by all and not resisted.

THE BENEFITS OF DELEGATION

The benefits of effective delegation come in many shapes and sizes. You will find that your administrative costs come down because people are working more efficiently and your business is more streamlined. You will also find that you have more time to focus on key issues because you've created that extra time for yourself. Your business should become more profitable because it is being run more effectively.

REAL-LIFE STORY

A manager of an insurance brokerage firm found that it was becoming increasingly difficult to cope with both managing his busy office, which he hated doing, and securing the big insurance contracts, which he loved. His poor management of his workload was creating delays in the office, which caused problems for the staff and disrupted everybody's busy week. He decided to promote one of his more senior and capable staff to the position of office manager. This is what he has to say:

'The new office manager felt that she was being entrusted with an important task and gladly took the job on, dealing with matters diligently and successfully. I never set the business up because I loved admin, and my new office manager is better at it than me. She welcomed her

responsibilities and flourished in her new role, leaving me to get on with chasing those big deals and growing the business. If I had not acted when I did, the status quo would have damaged my business. I just had to recognise the different strengths and weaknesses of the team and make sure we used them to the benefit of the business.'

BARRIERS TO DELEGATION

There are, of course, many reasons why people feel disinclined to delegate. Here are a few of the most common:

- **Perfectionism** – many entrepreneurs are perfectionists. Perfectionists are analytical and meticulous in the way they go about their business. They do not think that others will do the job as well as they can, and as a result they are loath to let others try. This results in them becoming overwhelmed with work – which, of course, is unsatisfactory for them because they are unable to do anything as well as they would like, while their employees become dissatisfied because they do not feel they are trusted. This is counter-productive for the business, because it will be inefficient.

- **Emotional involvement** – some entrepreneurs are artistically and/or emotionally involved with their business – for example artists, designers, craft workers and the like. It is very difficult for someone who cares a great deal about the product or service they provide to be objective about the mechanics of running the business. They see the product or service as far more important than administration, which is neglected because it always comes second.

- **Insecurity** – newly self-employed are often (and quite understandably) insecure or hesitant in their new role. However, this insecurity fuels a lack of trust in others or a lack of confidence in their own management skills, which in turn creates problems for their business. They must overcome this barrier and learn to trust people and trust themselves so that their business can grow.

- **Don't touch my baby!** – some entrepreneurs may have spent many years designing or inventing a product and, as a result, are extremely reluctant to allow others to come to their aid. This can be called the 'don't touch my baby' barrier, and it may be one of the hardest to overcome. Once again, though, it is an issue of the owner-manager's trust in others and of coming to the understanding that they must be as committed to growing the business and to their staff as they are to their invention.

Do any of these sound like you? If so, take heed! Delegation is not something you can opt out of if your business is going to grow and be successful.

MANAGING PEOPLE

One of the greatest challenges to anyone in business is getting the best out of their staff. It is crucial for the health of your business that you get it right and it can be an upsetting experience for everyone when you get it wrong. Learning how to delegate is a key step in the process of learning how to manage people well – but it's not the only thing you need to know. As your business grows, good management skills become more and more important. In this section, one small business owner uses his experience to offer some advice on stepping up your management skills.

'If you approach the business of taking on staff with care, it can be a rich and rewarding experience. You get a real sense of achievement when your team is working as a solid unit and everyone is pulling together.'

Mike, landscape garden
and nursery entrepreneur

Mike started his successful South Devon landscape garden and nursery business 10 years ago. He and his and wife Denise, have survived intense competition, dreadful winters and recession. They now own a thriving business with 12 employees. Mike focuses on the business's three landscaping teams that create and maintain some of the finest private gardens in the South-West and Denise runs the busy nursery, which is open to the public. To coin Mike's phrase, managing staff has not 'always been a bed of roses' – but he has learned the hard way and coped. He has come up with 10 golden rules to help you step up the pace of your growing business by taking on staff. These rules could be applied to any ambitious self-employed person.

STEPPING UP – 10 GOLDEN RULES FOR MANAGING PEOPLE

Start with Mike's three priorities. (1) *Select big customers with care* because bad customers, who don't pay do not pay when you need them to, can be very bad for your cash flow and this has all sorts of negative impacts upon the health of the company. (2) C*hoose employees with care*. They are an essential ingredient for success and expansion. (3) Make sure there is e*nough capital* available for any proposed expansion. Make sure you analyse carefully at the outset to ensure that any expansion is properly funded.

Think carefully about the size of the business you wish to create. If expansion is not managed carefully and profitability is not monitored accurately, then your expansion will weaken control and the quality of your product or service, for a debatable increase in profits. In short, you must think carefully about the risks attached to expansion and whether it is going to be worth it in the long run.

Employing people creates a new and very different relationship. You are no longer workmates because you now have to convey authority and ensure that it is not resented. Instructions have to be detailed and 'pitched right', to ensure that they are sufficiently understood by those who have received them.

Passing the total of four employees means that your working relationships will change once again, because you may need to delegate some of your management responsibilities to a 'sub leader' and this involves a completely new set of delegation and management challenges.

Positive comments from customers about a job well done should be passed on to the employees concerned. Try to remember that everyone likes to get 'positive strokes', especially when they have made a special effort. Mike suggests a diary to record the week's customer feedback. *'You can refer to it at the end of the week'* he said, adding *'It's important to remember that employees don't want to just hear their boss being negative – praise when it's been earned, is good'*.

It is possible to be friends with your employees and indeed pleasant to socialise with them, but a certain distance must be maintained. *'You can't totally relax because you must not compromise yourself and lose respect'*, Mike explains. *'You must keep one careful eye on the business objective and if this balance between being sociable and being a manager is not maintained, it will be bad for business.'*

Never assume that the information and instructions you have given an employee will mean that the job will be done exactly as you imagined. You will need to check that your message has been understood on a regular basis, because people can interpret the clearest of instructions very differently.

Getting the job done will always be at the back of your mind, but don't let that obscure the need to give the job of managing people sufficient time. In Mike's case good 'weather windows' meant that sometimes he was so busy that he did not provide his employees or team manager with enough information; consequently he sometimes found that jobs were not done to his or a customer's satisfaction. He found that this was sometimes caused by the fact that he had made arrangements in a hurry and the reasons for his haste, had everything to do with the pressure he had been under to 'get the job done' at the time. Instructions must always be clear and sufficient time should always be given to ensure that they are understood properly by those you have delegated work to.

Until you know your employees well and can trust them to do the job as you would wish, you should supervise them closely. Your employee's idea of a carefully done job may be completely different to your own.

Problems with staff are bound to occur, whoever you are, so try not to take disagreements personally. Remember, you must stay focused. It is important that the manager says what needs to be said and is then able to negotiate so that everybody can work towards a settlement. You must all then start afresh as workmates once again. It is essential that the manager keeps everybody on board and makes sure that there is no bitterness in the team.

BODY LANGUAGE

Learning to read others' body language and to give out the right body language yourself can be a very useful management skill. It means you can give off an air of authority, and it will also make you sensitive to when your employees (or customers for that matter) might be feeling vulnerable or upset – which means you will be quicker to anticipate and respond to situations in an effective way. Take a look at the following list to learn how to read the signs:

- Brisk, erect walk = confidence

- Walking with hands in pockets, shoulders hunched = dejection

- Standing with hands on hips = readiness or aggression

- Sitting with legs crossed, foot kicking slightly = boredom

- Sitting with hands clasped behind head, legs crossed = confidence, superiority

- Locked ankles = apprehension

- Arms crossed on chest = defensiveness

- Hands clasped behind back = anger, frustration, apprehension

- Hand to cheek = evaluation, thinking

- Stroking chin = trying to make a decision

- Touching, slightly rubbing nose = rejection, doubt, lying

- Rubbing the eye = doubt, disbelief

- Pinching bridge of nose, eyes closed = negative evaluation

- Pulling or tugging at ear = indecision

- Rubbing hands = anticipation

- Open palm = sincerity, openness, innocence

- Biting nails = insecurity, nervousness

- Tapping or drumming of fingers = impatience

- Steepling fingers = authoritative

- Patting/fondling hair = lack of self-confidence, insecurity

- Head resting in hand, eyes downcast = boredom

- Tilted head = interest

- Looking down, face turned away = disbelief

Source: www.deltabravo.net/custody/body.php

CONCLUSION

Don't forget, the key to all successful relationships is respect. You should earn your staff's respect by treating them fairly, and they should earn yours by carrying out their work to the best of their abilities.

CHAPTER 6

Troubleshooting

There are many other issues that will need to be dealt with as your business grows and becomes more complex. This chapter covers a few of the areas not included in the previous chapters – including:

- Time management

- Choosing location and premises

- Recovering debt

- Avoiding the doldrums

- Looking after yourself.

All are key areas to consider on the road to self-employment.

TIME MANAGEMENT

Remember that hectic day described in the previous chapter, where you answered 12 phone calls, went to three meetings, dealt with seemingly infinite bits of paper, handled five queries, sorted two crises – and felt like you had achieved absolutely nothing productive? Does it still sound familiar? Well, as well as indicating that you need to delegate some of your workload, it also suggests that your time management could do with some improvement.

It doesn't matter what type of business you are in – the feeling that time is running away with you and that you're losing control is very unpleasant and leads to hasty decisions that can cost time and money you can ill afford. There's another point to consider, too: you probably started the business to give yourself *more* freedom, not less; to spend *more* time with your family, not less. If you don't manage your time, the business can turn into a big, time-greedy monster that starts running your life. This is sometimes known as the 'cuckoo complex' (because, like a cuckoo outgrows its adopted parents and takes over the whole nest, so your business outgrows the time you have and takes over your life).

But it doesn't have to be like this. Use the tips below to help you prioritise your work and master the art of efficient time management.

BEING CLOCKWISE

Clear your desk of unnecessary junk. Keeping your workplace tidy and free of interruptions will help you manage your time effectively, because you will avoid missing opportunities and losing information, which increase tension and cause problems that take you an age to solve.

Look at your personal and business horizons. Consider this scenario: you're boarding a plane, about to go on holiday and you bump into the pilot who, on being questioned about the flight, shrugs and says: 'No idea what the wind speed is, how much fuel we need or what our ETA is. Sorry!' Would you have confidence that you are going to arrive at your destination safely and on time? A bank manager or funding panel has the same feelings of doubt when faced with a business start-up candidate who has not carefully considered their business and personal objectives in one, two or three years' time and what strategy they plan to adopt to achieve them.

Optimise your use of time. Needless meetings, pointless telephone calls, useless paperwork and constant 'fire-fighting' distract you and waste valuable time. One way to deal with paperwork is called the 'red dot test', where a fat red marker pen is used to dot paperwork every time it is picked up. If, at the end of the week, your paperwork looks like it has chicken pox, you know you're not handling paperwork effectively. Don't pick up any paper unless you act on it, refer it to someone else to deal with or throw it away.

Calendars, diaries and year planners are indispensable. A diary is a constantly changing record of your future action. Year planners are an excellent means of being able to see the coming year at a glance, enabling you to map out your future activity.

Keep using action plans. Once you have decided on your business and personal goals, you must devise a means of achieving them. Action plans will enable you to define measured and achievable steps towards realising your objectives. These objectives must be prioritised, constantly updated and revised.

Where possible, delegate – and avoid being a perfectionist, which can be expensive and can damage profitability.

Identify and eliminate the small business 'time bandits' such as time-wasters, unnecessary diversions and non-vital tasks, all of which will consume time and reduce effectiveness.

Set SMART goals (Simple, Measurable, Achievable and Relevant within an agreed Timescale) to help you remain focused and bring a sense of achievement and reality to your business's progress.

Evaluate meetings and projects so that lessons can be learned. It's important for you to be the one who monitors your performance, not your bank manager.

These are just few of the many clockwise tips you can choose from. They can all make a difference to a small business. Your guiding principle as you journey towards profitability should be: 'I am in control.'

If you need to remind yourself about the need to manage your time, do what a newly converted clockwise entrepreneur once did. She wrote 'I am in control' on her office clock face – customers always commented on it and the message proved a useful reminder for her to always try to be clockwise, whatever type of pressure she felt she was under. It even worked on those busy, hectic days when she felt that she could almost hear the cuckoo complex calling in the distance.

And remember, there are plenty of training options and advisory channels open to help you cope. It's just a question of knowing where to look and what to look for. Enterprise Agencies, Business Link, colleges and libraries can all be excellent sources of advice on how to manage your time more effectively – see the Resources section for more details.

FASCINATING FACTS

The self-employed are a hard-working bunch. In March–May 2006, 34% of self-employed people worked more than 45 hours per week.
Source: Office for National Statistics, Labour Force Survey

LOCATION AND PREMISES

Many entrepreneurs start their businesses by working from home and can avoid the issue of premises – at least until their business has expanded enough to warrant renting an office. The case study at the end of the introduction, however, provides a good example of what happens if you avoid facing up to the issues of getting premises. If you plan to work in certain sectors (for example retail), however, premises may be one of the first things you need to sort out before your business can even begin to trade.

Selecting the ideal premises is possibly one of the most important business decisions that you are going to face. It can have a tremendous impact on its future success – this applies both to start-ups and to existing businesses facing expansion.

CHOOSING A LOCATION
The first thing you need to think about is location – this is absolutely critical to the future success of any business, retail or otherwise.

For instance, if small a café is fifty yards away from the main pedestrian area, it can have a disastrous effect on turnover. Similarly, an office located in the middle of nowhere can limit your ability to recruit employees, and dingy-looking offices may make you look unprofessional and damage your reputation. And if you're miles away from your suppliers, you may have to pay higher transport costs.

If you are going to be using your premises to sell goods to passing trade, then the first thing to consider is **footfall**. Footfall is, literally, the number of people passing a certain point, and the best way to measure it is simply to observe how many people pass at various times of the day. You can make the measurement in a street, which will give you an idea of passing traffic in a certain location, or you can look at how many people go into a certain shop that may be similar to the one you are planning to open, which will give you an idea of how many potential customers you may have.

For example, one publican, when he was considering buying a pub, visited on several different evenings and at lunchtimes, before making a decision. He was watching customers and making notes on what they were buying, when they were buying it and how much was bought. He then fed this data into his business plan, which was thus based on reality, not assumptions.

You also need to think about the type of people that live in the area where the office is located. Are they the sort of customers you are looking for? Areas, and people who live in them, differ. You must ensure that your marketplace is where your business is. Choose the wrong location and force your customers to travel some distance to do business with you, and you will soon find that turnover drops, profitability slumps and customer numbers dwindle.

There are many other issues connected to location which may have an effect on your turnover. A good example is parking. One businessman commented 'I remember an office where I worked, which was near a college and, in term time, parking was always a problem, especially when an event took place'. Is parking going to be critical to your business's health? If so, you need to make sure there is enough available in the surrounding area.

CHOOSING YOUR PREMISES

Once you've decided on the general location you are looking for, it's time to start searching out the right kind of premises. Here are some questions to ask to help you make your selection:

- Which type of premises is for you? Easy in, easy out; long-term lease; or freehold? (see box below)

- If you are making a funding bid, does it impose any restrictions on your location?

- How much money can you spend on accommodation? Define a budget and stick to it

- What communication links are essential to your business? For instance, you may require a broadband connection to the internet, good road links to the office or public transport

- What planning permission or change of property use issues must be dealt with?

- Do you need storage? Analyse how much, and remember to account for future growth needs

- Is there enough space for future expansion in the office? (Size is important)

- Are there are any health and safety matters that need to be dealt with when you take on these premises?

- Will there be any costs associated with improving disabled access to observe the government's access rules and regulations?

- What other hidden costs might there be? Have you considered and checked what your local council's business rate charges are going to be? How high are the utility charges (electricity, telephone, etc)? What are the insurance costs going to be?

- What other issues must be considered? Do you need parking, a managed reception, conference rooms or some form of security for the building?

THREE TYPES OF PREMISES

There are three types of premises: freehold, leased and easy in, easy out.

Freehold

A freehold property is one that is owned outright. There are the usual planning restrictions, but essentially the building is yours until you decide to sell it. Most small businesses will find the high cost of purchasing freehold premises prohibitive; however, if you find yourself in a position to take this route, make sure that you seek legal advice. You may also need to get a surveyor to look at the property. Buying is a big step and, although you have more control over what may become an appreciating asset, you will also be fully responsible for all expenses, maintenance and repairs.

Lease

A lease is a contract by which a property is conveyed to a person for a specific period, usually in exchange for rent. The lease is the legal instrument by which such property is conveyed. Leases usually run for a significant of time and considerable notice must be given if you plan to move out. Business Link describes a lease as being an agreement 'where you might also allow the rent to be reviewed periodically'. It also points out on its website (www.businesslink.gov.uk) that upfront costs for leasing premises are often relatively low, although you may pay a premium to purchase the lease, and may find yourself obliged to pay for future maintenance and repair costs as well as legal fees.

'Easy in, easy out' premises

Many accommodation providers supply small and medium-sized enterprises (SMEs) with affordable accommodation, easy in and easy out tenancy agreements and secure buildings, often with an onsite managed reception and access to meeting rooms. Often you only have to give one month's notice if circumstances change and you find you want to move out. As Mandy Lloyd, of The Millfields Trust, Plymouth, explains: 'Easy in, easy out lease agreements allow businesses to occupy premises without the risk of taking out a long-term lease when starting or expanding.'

Finding the right premises is tremendously important to the health of any small business. Get it right and you have a reasonably priced home for your growing company; get it wrong and you'll have an expensive burden that your firm can ill afford. So approach this subject with care and proceed with caution. Don't forget, there is plenty of help available. You are not alone out there.

RECOVERING DEBT

The biggest killer of small businesses is bad cash flow. This is where you find access to cash dwindling to the extent that you can't pay your bills, which obviously causes difficulties.

Late or non-payment of debt is a common and upsetting reality of business life, so if you are in business you should be ready for it because it comes out of the blue and will make you see red.

'I just wasn't prepared for this customer's reaction and all the hassle he caused me. Whatever I did, he seemed completely indifferent. It's almost as if he was used to being chased for money.'

Small business owner

However, there are some things that can be done to minimise the risk of encountering bad debt and, when it does occur, there is a process you can follow to give yourself the best chance of recovering your money.

THE BASICS

First, you need to make sure you have the basics in place. Start by sorting out your invoicing procedure. Cobweb's information factsheet states: 'Invoices are a formal record of trading between you and your customers, containing details of the goods or services that you have supplied and the prices you have charged. They are used for the basis of all financial management and accounting processes in a business, and are a key business tax record and proof of purchase.' Invoices should contain the following:

- An invoice number

- Your business name, address and VAT number (if you charge VAT)

- An issue date

- Your customer's name (or company name) and address

- A description of the quantity and type of goods or services supplied, along with the price charged, and the VAT amount (if you charge VAT)

- The payment terms for the invoice.

There are several different types of invoice:

- **Pro-forma invoice** – issued by the supplier and sent before delivery when you do not have credit. On receipt of payment, the goods are delivered

- **Standard invoice** – issued to confirm a deal, and what payment was agreed and the date by when it is to be paid

- **Credit note** – issued to cancel an original invoice, or when goods are returned or when an error has been made.

Organise your book-keeping so that your debtors are automatically warned, in writing, as to the increasing seriousness of their debt. Your invoices and terms of business must state clearly your credit terms and/or how long you are happy to wait for payment.

THE THREE STAGE PROCESS TO DEBT RECOVERY

It's almost certain that you will encounter late or non-payment sooner or later. There are various remedies available to a business with debtors who cannot, or will not, pay their bills. First, negotiation includes discussions on the phone, letters from you or your solicitor, reminders and statements. Second, there are alternative means of resolving disputes. Third, there is court action. Each of these stages is explained in more detail in the paragraphs below.

1. NEGOTIATION

Informal negotiation should always be your first course of action, especially if you want to continue doing business with the company or person. A telephone call or meeting is usually the most productive approach. You should reinforce your first approach with letters, faxes and E-mails. This creates a paper trail which can be used as evidence, should you need it later.

If the invoice is not paid by the end of the first period of credit (usually 30 days), then you should immediately send a second invoice, clearly labelled 'reminder'. Should this fail to get a response, write a polite but firm letter insisting on payment. In the final instance, if payment is still not forthcoming, you should ask a solicitor to write on your behalf, stating that you are considering legal action unless the matter is resolved within a specific period of time.

If several invoices to the same business are unpaid, you should, in addition to the above, issue regular statements detailing the unpaid invoice numbers, dates, and the amounts outstanding for the goods or services supplied.

You may be entitled to charge interest, and this can provide a strong incentive for the debtor to settle. However, this interest has to be agreed at the time the contract is made, and it would be wise to mention the interest charge in the terms and conditions of business. A letter pointing this out to the debtor may be helpful when pressing for payment.

2. ALTERNATIVE DISPUTE RESOLUTION

Should negotiation fail, you are entitled to seek redress through the legal system. However, courts are of the opinion that legal action should be the last resort, and these days they are actively encouraging alternatives such as arbitration and meditation – these schemes are collectively known as alternative dispute resolution (ADR). ADR is particularly useful when the debtor contests details of the debt, such as its amount, and the court may insist that parties attempt ADR before a judgment will be considered.

ADR services are often carried out by a specialist consultant who is a member of the Chartered Institute of Arbitrators and who may well charge you a fee for a legally binding conclusion. Both parties must have agreed to abide by the decision at the outset.

3. COURT ACTION

If you have not been able to recover the debt by negotiation and cannot agree ADR, you may feel you have no choice but to pursue the debtor through the County Court. If you do so, you will need to undertake a bit of research or take the advice of a professional such as a solicitor before you go any further.

Many solicitors offer free advice. Before you embark on court action you must be satisfied that the debtor is an individual or company with the means to pay any judgment. There is little point in 'throwing good money after bad' and pursuing someone who won't pay because they can't pay.

If you decide to commence a County Court claim, you can obtain the necessary forms from the Court Office. You set out your claim and attach copies of relevant correspondence, such as copy invoices, to the claim form. You will have to pay a fee. The Court will serve the claim form for you. The Court Office will also give you helpful leaflets. The leaflets and court forms are free of charge.

If the debtor does not acknowledge the claim form or seek to defend the claim within certain prescribed time limits, it should be possible for you take steps to obtain a default judgment then try to enforce the judgment and seek payment. If the debtor defends the claim, it may automatically be transferred to the debtor's home County Court.

If the claim is for £5000 or less, the Court will, on allocating the case, usually place it in the Small Claims Track. There are two other ways of pursuing a claim, these being the Fast Track (for claims between £5000 and £15,000) and the Multi Track (for claims in excess of £15,000). Whichever track the case goes into, the Court will manage the case and the evidence admitted. These figures may change, of course, as time passes.

If you are successful and obtain a judgment, you may then need to enforce it. This will involve further fees. You can apply for a Third Party Debt Order to secure money in the debtor's bank or building society account. It may be possible to secure a Charging Order against property owned by the debtor or in which he or she has a financial interest. You could obtain an order attaching an individual's earnings, so that you receive some of their wages to be put directly toward repaying the debt.

The judgment may also form the basis of proceedings to have the debtor declared bankrupt. You can also ask the Court to order the debtor to disclose details of their financial position.

TOP TOPS ON DEBT

- Agree credit terms and periods before you do business

- Issue statements, reminders and invoices promptly and regularly – many businesses will not pay an invoice until they receive a reminder

- Prevention is better than cure – check the credit record of your suppliers and customers against the Register of County Court Judgments (a small fee is charged)

- Check with the Insolvency Service to ensure your debtor is still in business before starting court actions

- If in any doubt, consult a qualified solicitor. Solicitors often have small business schemes that offer free initial consultations.

It is worth mentioning that other solutions to debt recovery exist – for example, you may wish to use a debt collection agency, factoring service or invoice discounting company. If you use a debt collection agency, make sure you choose one that offers court action at no extra cost if they fail at the 'letters and phonecalls' stage.

Recovering debt is a difficult part of the journey into self-employment but, like any trip, the ride will be less stressful with a little homework and good planning. The best motto for dealing with bad debt may be: 'Don't panic, and be prepared.' The Resources section at the end of the book contains a number of useful websites.

BEWARE THE DOLDRUMS!

'We were sailing along at a cracking pace and then found ourselves becalmed. I can't understand it.'
Businessman

WHAT ARE THE DOLDRUMS?

Many people successfully start a business only to encounter difficulties at a later point in time. A launch will take place amid a flurry of activity and publicity, and friends and family will rally round offering enthusiastic support, often becoming the first customers. The new entrepreneurs, carried along on the crest of a wave, think that it will always be like this, as they enjoy the hustle and bustle of a dream come true.

Then, suddenly, everything goes quiet, turnover plummets, silence reigns and profits dwindle to a minus figure. There doesn't appear to be a logical reason for this – after all, everything was going so well. It's not long before panic sets in and the dream starts to look a little more like a nightmare. This stage is known as the 'Doldrums', because of an analogy with sailing. The Doldrums, literally, is the region near the equator where the meeting of trade winds produces light, baffling winds and calms. The Doldrums are much feared by sailors as they can cause great problems in a journey that previously seemed to be plain sailing.

WHAT CAUSES THE DOLDRUMS?

There are plenty of potential causes – this is by no means a comprehensive list:

- If you meet with success early on, others will notice, and new competitors may arrive on your doorstep overnight in an attempt to capitalise on your success

- Your business may have a limited number of potential customers and you may meet saturation point earlier than you think

- Existing competitors may discount prices as a response to your arrival, resulting in a potentially unprofitable price war

- Newer arrivals may appear in the marketplace with eye-catching products or services.

STAYING AFLOAT

Don't panic! There are plenty of ways to make sure your business stays afloat and makes it through the Doldrums. First, you must try to be aware of the changes that are taking place in your chosen marketplace, and be willing to adapt and take advantage of new developments. This should enable you to:

- Diversify into new markets

- Advertise aggressively to counter competition

- Modify and improve your services or product

- Perhaps even consider acquisition and expansion.

There are some golden rules that apply to a small business as you grapple with the challenges of the early years – and the good news is that, having read most of this book, you should be familiar with them all. In brief, they are:

- **Good planning** – the enthusiasm with which people approach the start-up phase of a new business will often obscure the need to plan carefully. But determination alone is not enough to guarantee success without adequate research, good financial planning and a decent business plan. See Chapter 2 for more information.

- **Good promotion** – one of the common mistakes a new entrepreneur makes is to set about publicising the business enthusiastically at the start but then, once the customers start to arrive, to put less effort into promoting the business. The inevitable effect of this action is a delayed falling off of enquiries as a direct consequence of the reduction in promotional activity. See Chapter 3 for more information.

- **Good customer service** – it is wise to set aside some time every week to mail existing and new customers and to speak to as many people as you can on the phone. See Chapter 4 for more information.

- **Good management** – you may find that you are a great entrepreneur, but you may also find that you are not the best manager of people. See Chapter 5 for more information.

Even if everything seems to be going swimmingly, use the prospect of encountering the Doldrums as a spur to being ever-prepared and vigilant. It is never wise to be complacent because, at the very moment when you relax and start to feel that your future is assured, you might find that they suddenly (forgive the pun) take the wind right out of your sales!

SAFE PASSAGE – LOOKING AFTER YOURSELF

As you grapple with all the challenges of your first few years in business, try to remember that a solution to a problem could be just over the horizon. Above all, don't panic. Stress can cloud judgement and dampen enthusiasm, which in turn can lead to despondency. You need to make sure you look after yourself, as well as your customers and your staff!

One idea is to try to get away from it all when things seem to be getting on top of you. One owner-manager offers the following advice: 'Try taking a long walk or a short break away from home and business. Spend time with the family or talk things over with friends, sample some good wine or take in a good film.'

It's good to find time to switch off and recharge those batteries. You will be refreshed and ready once again to tackle the journey ahead. There are plenty of other people trying to deal with the same problems. Indeed, there is probably someone, somewhere, running the same type of business who has encountered the same problem. They may also have found a solution that they may be willing to share with you. Check websites, books and internet messageboards to see if you can find any solutions, and talk to other entrepreneurs, who are frequently very willing – and able – to help. After all, you're all in the same boat.

Help, in the form of training advice and funding, is always at hand in the form of organisations such as Enterprise Agencies, the Prince's Trust, Business Link and many others.

JOURNEY'S END

An imaginative and consistent approach to running a business that includes careful management and planning, a readiness to take advice on matters such as finance and an effective promotional strategy will ensure that you have a good chance of completing your journey into a secure self-employed future. So what next? The following chapter looks at some ways you can enhance your skills by taking relevant training and gaining enterprise experience, which will help you make your mind up before taking the plunge and give you a better chance of success when you do.

But first, take a look at the wise words from Enterprise Agency Business Advisers for those preparing to step out onto the road to self-employment.

WISE WORDS FROM THOSE WHO KNOW!
Steve Hutson, Business Adviser for Enterprise South Devon

'I would strongly suggest that any new entrepreneur should acquire a broad base of networking contacts that will benefit both the individual and their customers. They should be able to embrace change, and enthusiastically channel the energy that they have started their business with into the dealings they have within it – always conveying a positive message to the contacts made, both inside and outside of the business. It is important to remember that it takes years to get a good reputation but minutes to lose it.'

David Thompson, Business Adviser for Enterprise South Devon

'Great sales people are great questioners. Question your way into more sales but don't talk your way out of them!

'Remember: if you supply what the customer needs, you'll make a living; but give them what they want and you'll make a fortune.

'Think of stock as £50 notes plastered round the room. Check it regularly, review it regularly and change it regularly.

'Be proud of your products and services, and charge as much as the market will stand. Do not be cheap.'

Sue Massingham, Regional Manager for Prime

'Don't be afraid to trust your intuition – it is more often right than wrong.'

CHAPTER 7

Training

DECISION TIME!

The previous chapters should have given you a clear idea of how to go about setting up your own business. Now it's time to reflect on whether or not working for yourself is really for you. Think about all the skills you're going to need – everything from debriefing staff to chasing unpaid debts. Are you ready to face the challenge? If the answer is yes, then great! You can jump in at the deep end by contacting enterprise agencies, writing a business plan, getting funding and setting up your business straight away.

If you're interested and excited at the prospect of self-employment, but concerned that you may not yet have all the skills you need, don't panic! You can take steps to prepare yourself by taking one of the many training courses on offer at a further or higher education institution, or by getting involved in some relevant work experience via your school.

This chapter will guide you through what's on offer. Each learning provider or support agency has summarised the support and training options they offer for budding entrepreneurs.

Don't forget that the further, higher and secondary education options could be modular, full or part-time; involve distance learning and so on. Make sure you get as much information as possible on how you might enter the world of self-employment and make sure the option you choose suits you. Solutions vary from region to region; you have to look at what is available near you.

FURTHER EDUCATION

Viv Gillespie, Principal of Plymouth College of Further Education, explains how attending a further education college can help young entrepreneurs pursue their self-employed goals:

'Colleges of further education have a significant and pivotal role to play in helping aspiring young entrepreneurs to successfully pursue their employment goals, including those who are ultimately seeking self-employment. The range of vocational provision available at colleges like mine is integral to preparing students for their future employment, for helping them within their current careers or alternatively for those individuals seeking to change career direction.

'Self-employment is increasingly becoming a popular route and many of our mainstream courses include some consideration of the opportunities and challenges presented by this employment route. With most of our staff having significant industrial or commercial experience they are able to provide our students with practical, hands-on advice. Of course we also offer courses for individuals who are specifically seeking to start their own business and we work closely with the various enterprise agencies (both business and social) and local community organisations to provide convenient, local opportunities for budding entrepreneurs to receive comprehensive and supportive advice, training, education and mentoring.'

So what sort of courses might be of interest to those hoping to work for themselves? The box below outlines a few to look out for.

FE COURSES FOR BUDDING ENTREPRENEURS
Foundation degree (FdA) in Business or in Business and Information Communication Technology (ICT)

- **Timescale** – two years full-time or three years part-time

- **Description** – designed to provide a high-level broad-based business education or in business and ICT, for the purpose of progressing directly to careers in a wide range of business and management contexts or to complete a university-based degree. You may be given the option to specialise in areas like management, public sector management or marketing

- **What it can lead to** – on successful completion the student may progress to: (i) the final year of a BA(Hons) Business Administration degree; (ii) the second year of other business-related honours degree programmes; (iii) the final year of business honours degree programmes; (iv) a wide range of careers in business, management, personnel, marketing, finance, accounting and public administration

- **Requirements** – candidates will need one of the following: (i) 60 UCAS tariff points – any combination; (ii) a BTEC national diploma; (iii) an NVQ level; (iv) equivalent qualifications; (v) relevant work experience

Business Higher National Certificate (HNC)

- **Timescale** – part-time – distance learning for up to two years

- **Description** – each module of the qualification requires study of distance learning material and contact with a tutor. The programme may cover: (i) business finance; (ii) business environment; (iii) marketing; (iv) organisational behaviour; (v) quantitative methods

- **What it can lead to** – successful students can convert this qualification to a Business Foundation Degree by completing additional modules

● **Requirements** – candidates should have one of the following: (i) one A level (including A levels in applied subjects; (ii) a BTEC national diploma or certificate; (iii) relevant work experience

Business Awareness and Advanced Professional Study (CIPD)

● **Timescale** – this is a flexible learning programme which is structured around a series of one-day workshops (usually eight), written materials and tutor support

● **Description** – the course covers study skills, thinking skills, introduction to strategic management, introduction to statistical and financial information, introduction to strategic business context and continuous professional development

● **What it can lead to** – successful completion of this programme may lead to progression to the CIPD Professional Development Scheme

● **Requirements** – candidates would need to satisfy the college that they have the ability to successfully study at this level and the commitment to manage their own learning. Students normally complete the Certificate in Personnel Practice (which is a foundation level programme equivalent to NVQ/SVQ Level 3 in Personnel Support), prior to commencement of this programme

For a detailed list of the further education courses and entry requirements, take a look at the *Directory of University and College Entrance 2007–8*, published by Trotman.

HIGHER EDUCATION

A broad range of relevant courses are offered at higher education institutions throughout the country. Those that are relevant may include:

- Accountancy and Finance

- Business Administration

- Business Studies

- Human Resource Management

- Marketing and Public Relations

- Operations, Logistics, Supply Chain and Retail Management.

Take a look at *Trotman's Green Guides: Business Courses* (published by Trotman) for a detailed list of higher education courses and entry requirements. You may find that there are also other enterprise opportunities available at your university. The box below gives a sample of the kind of opportunities available at just one higher education institution.

REAL-LIFE EXAMPLE: PLYMOUTH UNIVERSITY

Dr Susan Boulton works in the Research and Innovation department of the University of Plymouth. She gives the following overview of the provision at her university:

'My role within the university is to encourage and support a culture of entrepreneurialism amongst our staff and students. We offer our young entrepreneurs a number of opportunities, including the following:

- Workshop programme

- Business plan competition

- One-to-one surgeries

- Specialist workshops

- Mentoring

- Proof of concept funding.

'Entrepreneurship is seen as a crucial means by which new ideas, novel approaches and advanced technologies are introduced continuously into business and the marketplace.

'Staff and students are supported in developing their business ideas through the entrepreneurship programme. The programme consists of interactive workshops equipping students and staff with practical entrepreneurial and enterprise skills along with the opportunity to access professional advice on how to set up and run your own business.'

There is also a Business Ideas Challenge, which runs alongside the workshop programme. As a University of Plymouth spokesman explains, the programme was 'established in support of new business ideas and business ventures. It offers young entrepreneurs the opportunity to turn their idea into a reality by providing professional advice, pre-start-up funds and high profile exposure to potential investors. The annual competition offers a total prize package worth over £30,000 in cash and in-kind support from its sponsors.'

Over the last three and half years, Plymouth has supported around 500 staff and students in developing their ideas. Here are a few examples of students who have benefited from the programme:

'I attended the Spring 2006 Entrepreneurship Workshop series. I found them to be lively and stimulating, with plenty of opportunity for interaction with the presenters – a good basis for setting up my own business in the future. I particularly liked the fact that the presenters were mainly professionals, with valuable current experience in the business world. The series has inspired me to help establish a student entrepreneur society at Plymouth next term.'
Miss Dan Li, 2nd year Business School student from China

'The workshops were diverse and thought-provoking, covering a wide range of subjects. The guest speakers were especially informative, adding a professional dimension to the real world of business. Overall, by the end of the series I found that I had a much more realistic view of commercial opportunities which will continue to inform my ongoing interests.'

Deborah Branton, Programme Administrator
at the Faculty of Education

SECONDARY SCHOOLS

You might think that school is not the place to learn about business and industry – but you would be wrong. There have always been plenty of opportunities to develop entrepreneurial skills – for example:

- Running school fairs at Christmas and summer

- Raising money for school trips of for the school charity

- Work experience – organised via your school careers teacher

- Young enterprise – see www.youngenterprise.org.uk for more information

- Education business partnerships (where businesses work alongside schools to give students the chance to participate in 'real business' – for more information, see www.nebpn.org).

However, in recent years even more opportunities have been developed as a result of the increasing prominence of the idea of 'work related learning'. By the end of Key Stage 4, each student should have spent a total of five days on a combination of the following:

- Work with local employers

- Meeting people from different occupations

- Careers advice and interviews.

The Government has also provided funding to every school for 'enterprise education' to help develop students' enterprise skills, skills for business and financial capability. In order to get access to this money, students have to 'plan, organise, carry out and evaluate' an enterprising activity. One secondary school representative explains: 'The activities can take place in curriculum time (although national curriculum constraints sometimes make this tricky) or in off-timetable activities – for example through visits and visitors and, most importantly, through students being encouraged to take the initiative and set up an enterprise of their own.

'The result is that a plethora of organisations now exists, offering activities that will help schools to spend the money! School Inspections will now include enterprise education and work related learning in their remit. Opportunities and developments will be widely varied across schools and colleges, depending on how the development is managed and supported internally.'

JUMPING IN AT THE DEEP END

If you fancy taking the plunge and starting up your business right away, then there is plenty of help out there. Andrew Ashley, Managing Director of Enterprise Plymouth Limited explains how the Business Support Sector can help:

'Enterprise agencies' close links with central, regional and local government are used to help people into self-employment and assist small and medium-sized businesses to expand in a viable and sustainable way. The main function is to provide information, business advice, coaching, finance, training and support to businesses employing fewer than 25 people. This is done by deploying people with experience of managing businesses in many sectors, who make themselves available at no cost to the business they are supporting.

'Special provision has always been made for young people, because it is they who often have the greater need due to the fast-changing world in which we live. They find the expertise of business men and women valuable, as they have not had the experiences they find in those people who are sent to advise them.'

Take a look at the Resources chapter to find the organisations that can help you.

GO FOR IT!

In many ways self-employment is a very creative thing and if you go about the process of being in business with determination and vigour, anything is possible. If you like the idea of working for yourself and choose to make this journey towards self-employment, then this book should help ensure that you follow the quickest route to profitability and success. Making to move into working for yourself can change your life – so go for it!

CHAPTER 8

Resources

GENERAL

ADAS Agricultural Advisory Service
Tel: 0845 766 0085
Web: www.adas.co.uk
A provider of environmental and rural solutions and policy advice.

Advice Guide
Web: www.adviceguide.co.uk
A web based directory of advice providers.

Advisory, Conciliation and Arbitration Service
Tel: 0845 747 4747
Web: www.acas.org.uk
Organisation providing up-to-date information, advice and training to improve employment relations.

Barclays/BT Business Profile Sheets
Web: www.business.barclays.co.uk
Barclays Bank business website.

Barclays/Freeserve Business Support
Web: www.clearlybusiness.com
Specialises in developing and providing software, information, best practice guides, news and services to small businesses.

Business Information Gateway
Web: www.rba.co.uk/sources/index.htm
Business information on the internet.

Business Link
Tel: 0845 600 9006
Web: www.businesslink.gov.uk
Provides practical advice for business.

Chartered Institute of Personnel and Development
Tel: 020 8612 6200
Web: www.cipd.co.uk
Professional body for those involved in the management and development of people.

Citizens Advice Bureau
Web: www.nacab.org.uk
A service to help people resolve legal, money and other problems by providing information from 3400 different locations in the UK.

Co-operatives Support UK
Tel: 0845 373 3616
Web: www.co-op-assist.co.uk
A workers' co-operative of specialist trainers and consultants.

Countryside Agency
Tel: 01242 521381
Web: www.countryside.gov.uk
A Government agency working to serve and enhance the English countryside.

Department for the Environment, Food and Rural Affairs (DEFRA)
Tel: 0845 933 5577
Web: www.defra.gov.uk
A Government department tasked with such issues as the environment and rural enconomy.

Department of Trade and Industry (DTi)

Web: www.dti.gov.uk
Tel: 020 7215 5000
A Government department working to create the conditions for business success.

Directgov

Web: www.direct.gov.uk
Central Office of Information (Government) internet service providing public service information and services online.

Federation of Small Businesses

Tel: 01253 336000
Web: www.fsb.org.uk
The UK's leading lobbying and benefits group for small businesses.

Forum of Private Business (FPB)

Tel: 0845 130 1722
Web: www.fpb.co.uk
Lobbies on behalf of small and medium-sized enterprises to create a better political and economic environment for business.

Health and Safety Executive

Tel: 0845 345 0055
Web: www.hse.gov.uk
A Government department responsible for health and safety regulation within the UK.

HSBC Business

Tel: 0800 731 8904
Web: www.hsbc.co.uk
HSBC bank's business department.

Inland Revenue

Web: www.inlandrevenue.gov.uk
The Government department responsible for collecting taxes.

Learning and Skills Council

Web: www.lsc.gov.uk
Government organisation to improve the skills of the workforce in the UK.

Livewire hotline
Tel: 0845 757 3252
Web: www.shell-livewire.org
Helps 16–30 years olds start and develop their own business and hosts a national competition for new business start-ups.

Lloyds Business
Tel: 0800 056 0056
Web: www.lloydstsbbusiness.com
Lloyds Bank's business department.

National Federation of Enterprise Agencies
Tel: 01234 354055
Web: www.nfea.com
The membership body for enterprise agencies.

NFEA Online Advice
Web: www.smallbusinessadvice.org.uk
Provides free professional advice using NFEA's enquiry service.

Prince's Trust
Tel: 0800 842842
Web: www.princes-trust.org.uk
Offers practical solutions to help young people get their lives working.

Small Business Service
Tel: 020 7215 5000
Web: www.sbs.gov.uk
A Government department ensuring Government support services are accessible, relevant and of high quality. Provides links to other Government support services.

Startups
Web: www.startups.co.uk
Website offering advice on setting up your own business, and annual awards programme rewarding the UK's best business start-ups.

Start in Business
Web: www.startinbusiness.co.uk
Information service for starting, buying or expanding a business.

MARKET RESEARCH

British Chambers of Commerce
Tel: 020 7654 5800
Web: www.britishchambers.org.uk
National body providing a network and voice for British business.

British Franchise Association
Tel: 01491 578050
Web: www.britishfranchise.org.uk
National body providing information about franchising.

British Library
Tel: 0870 444 1500
Web: www.bl.uk
National library of the UK and one of the world's greatest libraries.

British Market Research Bureau
Tel: 020 8433 4000
Web: www.bmrb.co.uk
National body which provides high quality research in specialist areas.

British Standards Institute
Tel: 020 8996 9000
Web: www.bsi.org.uk
Pioneers standards around the world.

British Tourist Authority
Web: www.visitbritain.com
Building the value of tourism to Britain.

BT Directory Enquiries
Tel: 118 500
Web: www.thephonebook.bt.com
Directory enquiry service.

Business Bureau of Information
Web: www.businessbureau-uk.co.uk
Small business information resource.

Business Magazine
Web: www.realbusiness.co.uk
Leading magazine for growing companies.

Business Zone News
Tel: 0117 915 3344
Web: www.businesszone.co.uk
Provides information and tools to help business people conduct their business online.

Cobweb Information for Business
Tel: 0191 461 8000
Web: www.cobwebinfo.com
Online service providing business tips, ideas, advice, guides, reports, news, know-how and opinions for small businesses.

Companies House
Tel: 0870 333 3636
Web: www.companieshouse.gov.uk
A Government department which incorporates and dissolves limited companies and provides company information to the public.

Confederation of British Industry
Tel: 020 7379 7400
Web: www.cbi.org.uk
Lobbying organisation for UK businesses on national and international issues.

Daily Telegraph
Tel: 020 7538 5000
Web: www.dailytelegraph.co.uk
National daily newspaper.

Financial Times
Tel: 020 7775 6248
Web: www.ft.com
National financial and business newspaper.

Government Search Facility
Web: www.open.gov.uk
Government online service which provides public service information.

Guardian
Tel: 020 7278 2332
Web: www.guardian.co.uk
National daily newspaper.

Innovation Unit
Web: www.innovation.gov.uk
Part of the Department of Trade and Industry providing support for small businesses as key sources of information.

Kelly's Business Directory
Web: www.kellysearch.com
Online advertising agency for industrial companies across the world.

Kompass Business Directory
Web: www.kompass.com
Leading provider of private collected business information – business to business search engine.

Kompass Directory UK
Web: www.kompass.co.uk
UK version of the above.

Mailing Lists Worldwide
Web: www.listsnow.com
Provides online access to mailing lists for marketing.

Market Research Society
Tel: 020 7490 4911
Web: www.mrs.org.uk
Association representing providers and users of market, social and opinion research.

Mintel Market Research
Tel: 020 7606 5932
Web: www.mintel.com
Global supplier of consumer, media and market research.

Office for National Statistics
Web: www.statistics.gov.uk
Government office which collates and provides national statistics.

Patents Office, Institute of
Tel: 020 7405 9450
Web: www.cipa.org.uk
Professional and examining body for patent agents in the UK.

Times
Tel: 020 7782 5000
Web: www.thetimes.co.uk
National daily newspaper.

SALES AND MARKETING

Advertising Standards Authority
Tel: 020 7492 2222
Web: www.asa.org.uk
Independent body set up by advertising industry to police the rules laid down in the advertising codes.

Association of Exhibition Organisers
Tel: 01442 873331
Web: www.aeo.org.uk
Association that offers assistance to any organisations or individuals involved in events and exhibitions.

Audit Bureau of Circulations
Tel: 01442 870800
Web: www.abc.org.uk
Provides access to circulation information for magazines, newspapers, exhibitions and directories within the UK and Republic of Ireland.

Data Protection Act
Tel: 01625 545745
Web: www.dataprotection.gov.uk
Government organisation that ensures public information is out in the open and personal information is properly protected.

Direct Marketing Association
Tel: 020 7291 3300
Web: www.dma.org.uk
Largest trade association in the marketing and communications sector.

Royal Mail Group plc
Web: www.royalmailgroup.com
Parent company of Royal Mail, Post Office and Parcelforce Worldwide. Website provides wealth of information related to these companies.

Telephone Preference Service
Web: www.tpsonline.org.uk
Organisation that helps to ensure telephone numbers are not available for sales calls. You need to register to access this service.

Thomsons Business Search
Web: www.businesssearch.co.uk
Provides access to directories database of 2 million UK business listings for sales and marketing.

UK Trade & Investment
Tel: 020 7215 8000
Web: www.tradeinvest.gov.uk
Government organisation which helps UK companies do business abroad.

UK Trade Fairs & Exhibitions
Web: www.exhibitions.co.uk
Official website for the UK exhibition industry.

Yellow Pages
Tel: 0800 605060
Web: www.yell.co.uk
Leading international business directory.

FINANCE AND FINANCIAL MANAGEMENT

Better Payment Practice Group
Web: www.payontime.co.uk
Co-operative forum of representatives of the business community and Government that seeks to improve the payment culture amongst organisations trading in the UK.

Helpline for the Newly Self-Employed
Tel: 0845 915 4515
Government run helpline giving advice on tax and National Insurance. You need to register your business here within the first three months or face a fine.

Her Majesty's Courts Service
Tel: 020 7189 2000 or 0845 456 8770
Web: www.hmcourts-service.gov.uk
Her Majesty's Courts Service administers civil, family and criminal courts in England and Wales.

Moneyclaim Online
Web: www.moneyclaim.gov.uk
Her Majesty's Courts online service for claimants and defendants.

BUSINESS PLAN

Robert Digby

Garden Services

Trading as

DIGGER'S GARDENING SERVICES

****

TABLE OF CONTENTS

---

* Appendices have not been included in Working for Yourself Uncovered.

CURRICULUM VITAE

Name: Robert Digby
Address: 21 Any Road, Anytown, Any County
Telephone: 01234 123456
Date of birth: 3 June 1980

PERSONAL PROFILE

A versatile and imaginative gardener with a businesslike approach to work. He has considerable experience in his line of work and shows resourcefulness and initiative. Polite and respectful, he is at ease with people at all levels and projects an air of discretion and respectability.

SUMMARY OF SKILLS AND EXPERIENCE

- Three years' training at Halwell Agricultural College gaining Advanced National Certificate in Horticulture

- Five years' experience working as part of a team of gardeners on a large country estate

- Extensive knowledge of landscaping and land husbandry

- Extensive plant knowledge

- Extensive experience in handling tools and machinery

- Diary organisation and time management

- Quotation and contract writing

EMPLOYMENT HISTORY

July 2003–date: Head gardener at Fine House Manor, Crediton

July 2001–July 2003: Under gardener at Fine House Manor, Crediton

July 2000–July 2001: Junior gardener at Fine House Manor, Crediton

TRAINING

Sept 1997–July 2000:   NVQ 3 Horticulture Course at Halwell
                       Agricultural College

ADDITIONAL INFORMATION

1998–date: Clean driving licence
March 1999:   Chainsaw Health and Safety course, Halwell
                       College

BUSINESS PROPOSAL

I am setting up a garden services business in my area covering a radius of approximately 30 miles. I gained an Advanced National Certificate in Horticultural at Halwell College and after five years' experience in gardening I feel confident enough to set up a gardening business of my own. I will operate from home, using my garage to store equipment.

My customers will mainly be homeowners with gardens within the Anytown area and my unique selling point (USP) will be my educational background, experience of horticultural issues, a reference from my previous employer and my competitive hourly rate.

OBJECTIVES

My objectives are:

1. To establish myself as a qualified, experienced, knowledgeable and affordable gardener within the first year. To have a client base of 10 and to make a net profit of £12,000

2. To enlarge the client base to 20 within the second year. To take on one employee and to have a turnover of £40,000

3. To expand the client base to 35 during the third year. To find premises within an industrial estate to store equipment. I also

anticipate needing another vehicle. My workforce will include two gardeners and a part-time administrator. I expect my turnover to be in the region of £70,000 thus exceeding the VAT threshold of £58,000.

STRENGTHS AND WEAKNESSES

Strengths: I have an Advanced National Certificate in Horticulture
           I am an experienced and knowledgeable gardener
           I am fit and healthy
           I have excellent interpersonal skills
           I am a good organiser and have excellent time management skills
           I am aware of health and safety issues relating to garden equipment
           I have a clean driving licence with full no claims

Weaknesses: I lack business experience
           I have no personal support
           I have limited funds to start the business
           I have no experience in managing people
           I have no marketing experience

MARKET RESEARCH

THE MARKET

My market will be anyone who needs assistance with maintaining their garden within a 30 mile radius of Anytown.

MARKET RESEARCH

To find out whether there was a demand for another service of this kind in my area I carried out a survey by posting a questionnaire of eight questions through 100 local letterboxes. The results were very interesting and I attach a copy of them.*

---

* *These have not been included in* Working for Yourself Uncovered.

I then spoke to some of the respondents on the telephone. They were keen for me to assist them with their gardens as there appears to be a shortage of qualified and affordable gardeners in this area.

COMPETITION
After discussions with people in the course of carrying out the survey, I looked at five other garden services within the area. I found they were all quite expensive, only one was qualified and they were all booked up with other clients for several months ahead.

This information confirmed that, despite there being plenty of competition, there is still a demand for this kind of service within my area.

EQUIPMENT
I have already built up quite a lot of tools and equipment since I was at college. I will need a truck and a few more specialist tools. I have received a number of quotations and calculated that the total amount need will be £8075, which will be included in my start-up costs.

SUPPLIERS
I have researched into the best suppliers for consumables and these are A N Other Garden Supplies, based in Anytown and ABC Garden Supplies based in Anothertown. They can provide good quality items such as lawn feeds, fertilizers and weedkillers at competitive prices. I have experience of using these suppliers through past employment and am satisfied with their reliability. Both are able to offer a quick delivery service, and neither apply a minimum order level, so I will not need to keep large amounts of stock. I will have to pay on a pro forma basis initially, but after three months will be able to have 30 days credit.

Questionnaire for Robert Digby – Digger's Garden Services

I am setting up a garden services business within the Anytown area and would appreciate your help in completing my market research. It would be a great help to me if you could spare me a few moments and kindly answer the following questions and return the questionnaire to me in the enclosed prepaid envelope.

1. Do you require the services of a gardener?   Y/N

2. If yes, how often would you require this service?

   Once a week   Y/N

   Once a month   Y/N

   Twice a year   Y/N

3. How much would you be prepared to pay per hour for this service?

Low	Mid	High
☐	☐	☐
£5–£10 per hour	£11–£15 per hour	£16–£20 per hour

4. Where would you look for a gardener (please tick any number of choices)?

   ☐ Local paper

   ☐ *Yellow Pages*

   ☐ Recommendation

   ☐ Local notice boards (eg library, post office, village shop)

   ☐ Other

5. Would you like a quote?   Y/N

6. Please give below your name, address and telephone number
   and I will call you to make an appointment to come and see you.

Name: ....

Address: ....

....

....

Tel No: ....

Additional Comments ....

....

....

....

MARKETING

DISTRIBUTION AND SELLING

I have created a wall map of the area I will be covering and I know
the area well having lived here for the past 15 years. My research
indicated that there is a demand for my services within the 30 mile
radius of Anytown originally defined at the outset of this business
plan. I shall initially follow up those responses from my market
research.

PRICING

Response to my original suggestion of £10.00 per hour for this
service has been positive and I will endeavour to keep supplies at a
low figure.

PROMOTIONAL STRATEGY
My promotional strategy will be as follows:

- I shall have signs placed on my work vehicle

- I shall carry out another leaflet drop to suitable properties in the area with gardens; this time the leaflet will be in the form of a flyer advertising my services. The leaflet drop will be made in batches of 250, with a week in between, to allow time to pursue new leads

- I shall place a card or flyer in local garden shops and centres

- If it proves necessary, I shall place a card on local boards (eg newsagents)

- If necessary I shall start a regular fund for advertising (budget of £50 per month) in the *Anytown Gazette* and local free papers, and will monitor success to identify the best places to advertise in the future.

LEGALITIES

INSURANCES

- Public Liability Insurance

- Employer's Liability Insurance

- Vehicle Insurance

- All risk insurance for tools to a value of £5000

- Contents insurance for the premises.

I have obtained several quotes and have chosen a comprehensive policy, covering all the above at a cost of £600 per annum.

LICENCES AND OTHER STANDARDS

Consumer legislation refers to the sale of goods, supply of goods and services etc.

HEALTH AND SAFETY

I have a relevant certificate for attending a health and safety course for chainsaw work. I intend to use a health and safety policy although I won't have five or more employees in the first year. Risk assessment will take place for every new client/garden undertaken and the appropriate training and protective clothing will be supplied to all staff.

TERMS AND CONDITIONS OF PAYMENT

Terms of payment will be agreed before the job commences. The terms will vary according to the type of job, whether it is regular job or a one-off and, if it is a one-off, how long it takes.

Regular jobs will be payable weekly or monthly on submission of an invoice, by either cash or cheque. At this stage I do not think it appropriate to have credit and debit card facilities.

CONTRACTS

Contracts will be issued depending on the nature of the job. Regular garden maintenance will not require a contract. However a large specific job may well require both a quotation and a contract and these will be issued and agreed with the client before the job commences.

PREMISES

For the first two years I will run the business from home, storing tools and equipment in my garage. I do not anticipate extra visitors and when I take on an employee in the second year I will still operate with only one vehicle.

If the business goes well I hope to find an industrial estate unit in the third year for storing tools and equipment and running an office.

FORM OF BUSINESS

I will operate as a sole trader.